T0395780

Ghost Food

Ghost Food

75 Spooky, Fun, and Frightening Halloween-Inspired Sweet Treats

CAYLA GALLAGHER

Skyhorse Publishing

Skyhorse Publishing books may be purchased in bulk at special discounts for sales promotion, corporate gifts, fund-raising, or educational purposes. Special editions can also be created to specifications. For details, contact the Special Sales Department, Skyhorse Publishing, 307 West 36th Street, 11th Floor, New York, NY 10018 or info@skyhorsepublishing.com.

Skyhorse® and Skyhorse Publishing® are registered trademarks of Skyhorse Publishing, Inc.®, a Delaware corporation.

Visit our website at www.skyhorsepublishing.com.

10 9 8 7 6 5 4 3 2 1

Library of Congress Cataloging-in-Publication Data is available on file.

Cover design by Kai Texel
Cover illustrations courtesy of Getty Images

Skyhorse ISBN: 978-1-5107-8261-7 | Scholastic ISBN: 978-1-5107-8458-1
Ebook ISBN: 978-1-5107-8262-4

Printed in China

Contents

Haunted Mansion

S'mores Marshmallow Ghost Tart

Crust:
6 ounces graham crackers
5 tablespoons unsalted butter, melted

Chocolate ganache:
12 ounces semisweet chocolate
¼ cup unsalted butter
1 cup heavy cream, hot

Ghosts:
4 egg whites, room temperature
1 cup granulated sugar
¼ teaspoon vanilla extract
⅓ cup DIY Candy Eyes (page 91)

Make the crust:
1. Crumble the graham crackers by pulsing them in a food processor or crushing them in a Ziploc bag.

2. Mix them with the melted butter until ful y incorporated and they feel like damp sand.

3. Press the mixture into a 14-inch rectangular tart pan with a removable bottom. Press the sides in first, then press the remaining mixture into the bottom of the pan.

4. Place the tart crust into the fridge to chill, for about 30 minutes.

Make the ganache:
1. Finely chop the chocolate and place it in a large microwave-safe bowl. Slice the butter into a couple pieces and sprinkle them on top.

2. Pour the hot cream on top and let sit for 5 minutes, then give it a stir. If the chocolate hasn't fully melted, microwave it for 30-second intervals until melted, making sure to stir at each interval.

3. Pour the ganache into the pan and smooth the surface. Return the tart to the fridge for the ganache to set, about 2 hours. You can also leave it in the fridge overnight and continue with the ghosts the following day.

Make the ghosts:
1. In a large bowl, beat the egg whites with an electric mixer until frothy. Slowly add the sugar while continuing to mix at medium-high speed. Keep beating until the meringue is no longer gritty when rubbed between your fingers and holds stiff peaks. Then add the vanilla extract and mix until combined.

2. Spoon the meringue into a piping bag fitted with a large round piping tip.

3. Pipe ghosts onto the tart. I fit 3 ghosts per row. Once all of the ghosts have been piped use a tweezer (or very careful fingers!) to stick the candy eyes onto the ghosts.

Serve:
1. Remove the sides of the tart pan by placing the tart on a couple jars and gently lowering the sides of the pan from the tart.

2. Then slice and enjoy!

Marshmallow Ghosts

If you don't have an edible ink pen, you can create the ghosts' faces by using a toothpick and a tiny amount of black food coloring!

Cooking spray
1/3 cup and 1/4 cup cold water, divided
2½ teaspoons powdered gelatin
1 cup sugar
1 teaspoon vanilla extract (or seeds
   from 1 vanilla bean)
1/4 cup cornstarch
1/4 cup confectioners' sugar
Black edible ink pen

1. Line a large baking sheet with parchment paper and spray with cooking spray. Set aside.

2. Pour 1/3 cup cold water into the bowl of an electric mixer and sprinkle the powdered gelatin on top. Let sit for 5 minutes.

3. Place the sugar and 1/4 cup cold water in a small pot and set to medium-high heat. Stir until the sugar has melted.

4. Attach a candy thermometer to the pot and boil the sugar until it reaches 238°F. Brush the sides of the pot with a wet pastry brush if sugar crystals stick to the sides. Remove the pot from the heat and stir until the sugar stops boiling.

5. Add the hot sugar to the gelatin and stir the mixture by hand whisking for a few minutes to slightly cool. Then beat with an electric mixer on medium-high speed for 8 to 10 minutes, until soft peaks form. Add the vanilla extract and mix until combined.

6. Spoon the marshmallow onto the greased baking sheet and smooth the surface. Allow it to dry for about 4 to 6 hours, or until it is no longer sticky to the touch, but still bouncy and not dried out.

7. Combine the cornstarch and confectioners' sugar in a small bowl and dust it over the entire surface of the marshmallow with a mesh sieve.

8. Dip a ghost-shaped cookie cutter into the remaining sugar mixture and cut out ghost shapes from the marshmallow. Dip the cookie cutter into the sugar mixture between each ghost, as it can get very sticky.

9. Dust the undersides and edges of the ghosts in the sugar mixture, then bounce them in the mesh sieve a couple times to remove any excess powder.

10. Use a black edible ink pen to draw faces onto the ghosts!

Mummy Pie

MAKES 1 (9-INCH) PIE

Piecrust:

2½ cups all-purpose flour
1 teaspoon salt
1 teaspoon sugar
1 cup cold unsalted butter, cut into cubes
¼–½ cup cold water

Filling and decorations:

8 cups fresh or frozen cherries, pitted
2 cups granulated sugar
½ cup cornstarch
Juice of ½ lemon
1 large egg, beaten
DIY Candy Eyes (page 91)

Make the piecrust:

1. Mix together the flour, salt, and sugar in a food processor. Add butter and pulse until it turns into a crumbly meal-like texture.

2. Transfer the mixture to a bowl and drizzle over the ice water. Mix with your hands until the dough sticks together when squished together.

3. Shape the dough into 2 disks and wrap them in plastic wrap. Place them in the refrigerator for 1 hour until firm.

Make the filling:

1. Place the cherries in a large pot and set to medium heat. Cook, stirring frequently, until the cherries have released their juice and are simmering, about 15 minutes.

2. In a separate bowl, combine the sugar and cornstarch. Add this to the cherries and stir until well combined.

3. Bring the cherry juice back up to a simmer and cook for 2 minutes, until thickened. Turn off the heat and add the lemon juice. Mix well, then allow to cool completely.

Assemble the pie:

1. Preheat the oven to 400°F. Roll 1 disk of piecrust out on a floured surface to ⅛-inch thick and about 11 inches wide. Gently drape this into a 9-inch pie plate and dock the base of the crust with a fork. This will help to release air while baking.

2. Spoon the cherry filling into the piecrust. It should just reach the top of the pie plate. If the filling looks a little too juicy, omit some of the juice—the more cherries the better!

(Continued . . .)

3. Roll out the second disk of dough to the same size as the first. Use a sharp knife to cut it into long strips. Vary the width of the strips—you want this to look like messy bandages.

4. Place the strips onto the pie in a slightly haphazard style, overlapping some edges and placing them at many angles. Press the edges of the strips onto the edges of the crust, sealing them together. Then use a sharp knife to trim off any excess dough from the edges of the pie plate.

5. Brush the strips and edges of the crust with the beaten egg.

6. Place the pie on a large baking sheet and bake for at least 35 minutes, until the crust is golden brown.

7. Allow it to cool at room temperature for about 30 minutes, then decorate with the candy eyes. They will soften over time in the juices of the pie, so if you are making this pie a couple days in advance, add the candy eyes just before serving.

Spiderweb Cake

MAKES 1 (6-INCH) CAKE

Cake batter:

2 cups all-purpose flour
2 cups sugar
¾ cup cocoa powder
2 teaspoons baking powder
1½ teaspoons baking soda
1 teaspoon salt
1 cup milk
½ cup vegetable oil
2 large eggs
2 teaspoons vanilla extract
1 cup boiling water

Buttercream and decorations:

3 cups unsalted butter, room
    temperature
2 teaspoons vanilla extract or seeds
    from 1 vanilla bean
6½ cups confectioners' sugar
Pink and black food coloring
2 cups mini marshmallows
2 Spider Cake Pops (page 13)

Bake the cake:

1. Place the flour, sugar, cocoa powder, baking powder, baking soda, and salt in a large bowl and mix together.

2. Add the milk, vegetable oil, eggs, and vanilla extract and mix with an electric mixer until combined.

3. Slowly add the boiling water and mix until well combined.

4. Grease and flour three 6-inch round baking pans.

5. Divide the batter evenly between the pans and bake at 350°F for 30 to 35 minutes, until a skewer inserted into the center comes out clean. Cool for 15 minutes in the pan, then turn onto a wire rack and cool completely.

Make the buttercream:

1. Beat the butter with an electric mixer until pale and fluffy. Add the vanilla extract and confectioners' sugar 1 cup at a time, beating with each addition.

2. Dye the buttercream bright pink.

Assembly:

1. Stack the cakes and spread some buttercream between each layer.

2. Coat the cake in a thin layer of buttercream, called a crumb coat. This will catch any excess cake crumbs. Chill the cake in the fridge for 20 minutes.

3. Coat the cake in a thick, generous layer of buttercream. Smooth the surface.

(Continued . . .)

4. Divide the remaining buttercream in half. Add a small amount of black food coloring to half of the buttercream to create a dark pink color. Add more black food coloring to the other bowl to make it a dark black color. Place the dark pink buttercream into a piping bag fitted with a large star-shaped piping tip. Place the black buttercream into a piping bag fitted with a small star-shaped piping tip.

5. Use the pink buttercream to pipe dollops around the base of the cake. Use the black buttercream to pipe a black garland around the top of the cake.

6. Place the cake in the fridge until the buttercream has chilled completely and is solid, about 1 hour. This is important! If you still need to make the Spider Cake Pops, now is a great time to do so.

7. Once the cake has fully chilled and the buttercream is hard to the touch, remove it from the fridge. Place the mini marshmallows in a microwave-safe bowl and heat for 30 seconds, or until melted.

8. Put on some latex gloves, then dip your hands into the marshmallow. Press your hands together, then pull them apart, stretching out the marshmallow so it looks like spiderwebs. Gently wrap the marshmallow around the cake.

9. Stick the spiders to the sticky web. If the spiders are a little too heavy, you can use a couple toothpicks to help keep them in place, particularly on the sides of the cake.

Spider Cake Pops

Cake pop base:
4 chocolate cupcakes (from
    Gravestone Cupcakes, page 43)
¾ cup chocolate chips, melted
¼ cup heavy cream
Pinch of salt

Legs and eyes:
2 cups melted chocolate chips
1 Tootsie Roll
DIY Candy Eyes (page 91)

Make the base:

1. Place the cupcakes in a large bowl and break them apart until they are a fine crumb.

2. In a separate bowl, combine the ¾ cup melted chocolate chips, heavy cream, and salt. Mix well. Add this to the cake crumbs and mix until fully combined. You can use an electric hand mixer if you like!

3. Shape the mixture into balls and place them on a baking sheet lined with plastic wrap. Make them all the same size or different sizes—whatever you like! Place the baking sheet in the fridge and chill the spiders until firm.

Make the legs and eyes:

1. While the spiders are chilling, make the legs by chopping the Tootsie Roll into smaller pieces. Place them on a microwave-safe plate and microwave for 20 to 30 seconds, until malleable. Roll the pieces into long, thin pieces and bend them into leg shapes. Set aside.

2. Once the spider bodies have chilled, dunk them one at a time into the melted chocolate chips. Use a fork to lift them out of the chocolate and allow any excess chocolate to drip off. Return them to the baking sheet and stick the legs to the sides of the spider. Stick two candy eyes (or eight!) onto the spider, then continue with the remaining spiders.

3. Return the baking sheet to the fridge for the spiders to set and the chocolate to harden. Then enjoy!

Fluffy Monster Cake

MAKES 1 (6-INCH) CAKE

Cake batter:

1 cup unsalted butter, room
temperature
2 cups sugar
3 teaspoons vanilla extract
6 large eggs
3 cups all-purpose flour
1 teaspoon baking soda
1 teaspoon salt
1½ cups sour cream
1 cup round, flat confetti sprinkles

Buttercream and decorations:

3 cups unsalted butter, room
temperature
2 teaspoons vanilla extract or seeds
from 1 vanilla bean
6½ cups confectioners' sugar
Green, purple, and black food
coloring
2 ice cream cones
2 mini marshmallows

Bake the cake:

1. Beat the butter and sugar with an electric mixer until pale and smooth. Add the vanilla extract and eggs one at a time, mixing with each addition.

2. In a separate bowl, combine the flour, baking soda, and salt. Add this to the batter in 2 additions, alternating with the sour cream. Add confetti sprinkles and mix until combined.

3. Spoon the batter into 3 greased and floured 6-inch round cake pans. Bake at 350°F for 30 minutes, or until a skewer inserted into the centers comes out clean. Cool completely.

Make the buttercream:

1. Beat the butter with an electric mixer until pale and fluffy. Add the vanilla extract and confectioners' sugar 1 cup at a time, beating with each addition.

2. Dye ¾ of the buttercream bright purple. Divide the remaining buttercream in half. Dye half of the buttercream bright green. Place the green buttercream into a piping bag fitted with a medium-sized round piping tip.

3. Divide the remaining buttercream in half again. Leave half white and dye the other half black. Place the white buttercream into a piping bag and snip off the end, creating a medium-sized round tip. Do the same with the black buttercream.

Assembly:

1. Stack the cakes and spread some purple buttercream between each layer.

(Continued . . .)

2. Coat the cake in a thin layer of buttercream, called a crumb coat. This will catch any excess cake crumbs. Chill the cake in the fridge for 20 minutes.

3. Spread a circle of white buttercream onto the front, center of the cake. This will be for the monster's eye. Pipe a large ring of green onto the white circle. Fill in the green circle with the black buttercream and smooth the surface of the black buttercream with a knife. Pipe a white dollop onto the top right of the eye as its sparkle!

4. Use a serrated knife to trim the ice cream cones to your desired height. Working with one cone at a time, use your finger to support one cone and pipe a swirl of green frosting on the cone, from base to tip. Place this onto the top of the cake and repeat with the other cone.

5. Place the remaining purple buttercream into a piping bag fitted with a large grass piping tip. Pipe fur all over the cake by holding the base of the piping tip close to the cake and squeezing the piping tip as you pull away from the cake. This will create a little tuft of fur! Cover the entire surface of the cake.

6. Lastly, stick 2 mini marshmallows below the eye as its teeth.

Haunted Cake

MAKES 1 (6-INCH) CAKE

Cake batter:

1 cup unsalted butter, room
    temperature
2 cups sugar
4 teaspoons vanilla extract
6 large eggs
3 cups all-purpose flour
1 teaspoon baking soda
1 teaspoon salt
1½ cups sour cream
Pink, blue, and purple food coloring

Buttercream and decorations:

3 cups unsalted butter, room
    temperature
2 teaspoons vanilla extract
6½ cups confectioners' sugar
Black, pink, purple, and blue food
    coloring
1 cup melted white candy melts
3 lollipop sticks
Yellow star sprinkles

Bake the cake:

1. Beat the butter and sugar with an electric mixer until pale and smooth. Add the vanilla extract and eggs one at a time, mixing with each addition.

2. In a separate bowl, combine the flour, baking soda, and salt. Add this to the batter in 2 additions, alternating with the sour cream. Divide the batter into 3 bowls. Dye it pink, blue, and purple.

3. Spoon all 3 shades of the batter into 3 greased and floured 6-inch round cake pans. Swirl it around in the pan to make a marble effect. Bake at 350°F for 30 minutes, or until a skewer inserted into the centers comes out clean. Cool completely.

Make the buttercream:

1. Beat the butter with an electric mixer until pale and fluffy. Add the vanilla extract and confectioners' sugar 1 cup at a time, beating with each addition.

2. Dye ¼ of the buttercream black and place it into a piping bag fitted with a small round piping tip.

Make the ghosts:

1. Line a baking sheet with parchment paper.

2. Place a dollop of white candy melts onto the parchment paper and smear the spoon downward, creating a ghost with a tail. Make ghosts of varying sizes and shapes.

3. Lay 3 lollipop sticks onto the parchment paper and make 3 larger ghosts that rest on top of the lollipop sticks.

4. Place the tray in the fridge for the ghosts to harden while you assemble the cake.

(Continued . . .)

Assembly:

1. Stack the cakes and spread some white buttercream between each layer.

2. Coat the cake in a thin layer of buttercream, called a crumb coat. This will catch any excess cake crumbs. Chill the cake in the fridge for 20 minutes.

3. Divide the remaining buttercream into 4 bowls. Leave 1 bowl white and dye the remaining bowls pink, purple, and blue. Set aside a couple tablespoons of pink buttercream and place it in a piping bag fitted with a small round piping tip. Place dollops of all 4 colors onto the cake and use a spatula to spread the buttercream over the entire surface of the cake, creating a multicolor effect.

4. Fit an empty piping bag with a medium-sized star-shaped piping tip. Spread all 4 shades of buttercream into the piping bag vertically, so it looks like the piping bag is striped. Squeeze the piping bag until all the colors begin to come out.

5. Pipe dollops around the base and top of the cake.

6. Stick the lollipop ghosts into the top of the cake and the other ghosts on the sides of the cake. Add little star accents as you like.

7. Use the black and pink buttercream from the piping bags to draw the ghosts' faces and cheeks.

Boo! Cake

Cake batter:
1 cup unsalted butter, room
    temperature
2 cups sugar
4 teaspoons vanilla bean paste
6 large eggs
3 cups all-purpose flour
1 teaspoon baking soda
1 teaspoon salt
1½ cups sour cream

Buttercream:
3 cups unsalted butter, room
    temperature
2 teaspoons vanilla bean paste
6½ cups confectioners' sugar
Black food coloring

Bake the cake:
1. Beat the butter and sugar with an electric mixer until pale and smooth. Add the vanilla bean paste and eggs one at a time, mixing with each addition.

2. In a separate bowl, combine the flour, baking soda, and salt. Add this to the batter in 2 additions, alternating with the sour cream.

3. Spoon the batter into 3 greased and floured 6-inch round cake pans. Bake at 350°F for 30 minutes, or until a skewer inserted into the centers comes out clean. Cool completely.

Make the buttercream:
1. Beat the butter with an electric mixer until pale and fluffy. Add the vanilla bean paste and confectioners' sugar 1 cup at a time, beating with each addition.

2. Dye ¼ of the buttercream black and place it into a piping bag fitted with a small round piping tip.

Assembly:
1. Stack the cakes and spread some white buttercream between each layer.

2. Coat the cake in a thin layer of buttercream, called a crumb coat. This will catch any excess cake crumbs. Chill the cake in the fridge for 20 minutes.

3. Then coat the cake in a smooth, generous layer of white buttercream.

4. Place the remaining white buttercream into a piping bag fitted with a large round piping tip.

5. Pipe little swirls on top of the cake. These are the ghosts!

6. Use the black buttercream to create the ghosts' faces and draw dots on the cake, as well as write "Boo!" on the front of the cake.

Hugging Ghost Cookies

Be sure to use a ghost cookie cutter that has arms!

Cookie dough:

2 cups all-purpose flour
¼ teaspoon salt
½ teaspoon baking powder
½ cup unsalted butter, room
    temperature
1 cup granulated sugar
2 tablespoons milk
1 large egg
½ teaspoon vanilla extract
12 orange peanut M&M's

Icing:

1 cup Royal Icing (page 177)
Black, brown, and green food
    coloring

Bake the cookies:

1. Preheat the oven to 350°F.

2. Mix together the flour, salt, and baking powder in a bowl. In a separate bowl, cream the butter and sugar with an electric mixer until it becomes light and fluffy.

3. Add the milk, egg, and vanilla extract. Mix until well combined, then add the flour mixture and mix until just combined.

4. Shape the dough into a ball and wrap in plastic wrap. Chill it in the fridge for 1 hour, until firm.

5. Roll the cookie dough out on a floured surface to ¼-inch thick. Use a ghost-shaped cookie cutter to cut out cookies and place them on a baking sheet lined with parchment paper.

6. Place an M&M's candy in the center of each of the ghosts' chests and fold the arms inward, so that they are "holding" them. Place the entire baking sheet in the fridge for the cookies to chill for 20 minutes.

7. Bake them for 10 minutes, until the edges are just starting to brown. Remove them from the oven, and if necessary, fold the arms back toward the center if they shifted during baking. Cool on the pan for 10 minutes, then transfer to a cooling rack and cool completely.

Decorate:

1. Dye ¾ of the Royal Icing black. Place it into a piping bag fitted with a small round piping tip.

2. Divide the remaining icing in half and dye it brown and green. Place them both into piping bags fitted with small round piping tips.

3. Pipe the ghosts' faces with the black icing, the pumpkin stems with the brown icing, and the vines with the green frosting.

4. Allow the frosting to dry completely before serving, about 1 hour.

Candy Corn Cake

What I love about candy corn is how quintessentially Halloween it is. What I do not like about candy corn is its taste. Luckily, we've found a workaround with this cake! Get all the cuteness of candy corn without the processed taste. This cake is a twist on my classic vanilla cake recipe, with the addition of pumpkin pie spice and maple syrup and substituting brown sugar for regular white sugar. It tastes fabulous!

Cake batter:

1 cup unsalted butter, room temperature
2 cups brown sugar
3 teaspoons vanilla extract
¼ cup maple syrup
6 large eggs
3 cups all-purpose flour
1 teaspoon baking soda
1 teaspoon salt
2 teaspoons pumpkin pie spice
1½ cups sour cream
Orange and yellow food coloring

Buttercream:

3 cups unsalted butter, room temperature
2 teaspoons vanilla extract or seeds from 1 vanilla bean
6½ cups confectioners' sugar
Orange and yellow food coloring

Bake the Cake:

1. Preheat oven to 350°F and grease and flour 3 (6-inch) round cake pans.

2. Beat the butter and brown sugar with an electric mixer until pale and smooth. Add the vanilla, maple syrup, and eggs one at a time, mixing with each addition.

3. In a separate bowl, combine the flour, baking soda, salt, and pumpkin pie spice. Add this to the batter in 2 additions, alternating with the sour cream. Divide the batter into 3 bowls. Leave one bowl white and dye the others each yellow and orange with a few drops of food coloring.

4. Spoon each different color of the batter into your prepared pans and bake for 30 minutes, or until a skewer inserted into the centers comes out clean. Cool completely.

Make the buttercream:

1. Beat the butter with an electric mixer until pale and fluffy. Add the vanilla extract and confectioners' sugar 1 cup at a time, beating with each addition.

Assembly:

1. Slice the tops and bottoms off the cakes to smooth the surface and remove any excess browning. Set aside the scraps from the white cake layer.

2. Stack the cakes, placing the yellow cake at the bottom, the orange in the middle, and the white cake on top. Spread ¼ cup buttercream between each layer.

3. Use a serrated knife to carve the cake into a candy corn shape, disregarding the top 2 or 3 inches where the point would be—we'll make that tip in the next step. Imagine a candy corn with a flat top—that's what you want to carve!

4. Crumble the remaining white cake scraps into fine crumbs. Add about 1 to 2 tablespoons of buttercream and mix well, until the cake crumbs retain their shape when rolled into a ball. You may need to add some extra buttercream (this is basically a cake pop mixture, and is a fabulous way to add shape to cakes without having to bake a whole extra layer). Place the mixture on top of the white layer and shape it into the top point of the candy corn.

5. Coat the cake in a thin layer of buttercream, called a crumb coat—this will catch any excess cake crumbs. Chill the cake in the refrigerator for 20 minutes.

6. Divide the remaining frosting into 3 bowls. Leave one bowl white and dye the remaining bowls orange and yellow with a bit of food coloring. Put all 3 colors in individual piping bags fitted with small, star-shaped piping tips.

7. Pipe the buttercream onto the cake in 3 large stripes, to look like a real candy corn!

Ghost Petits Fours

MAKES 14 GHOSTS

Cake batter:
½ cup unsalted butter, room
 temperature
1 cup sugar
2 large eggs
1½ cups flour
1 teaspoon baking powder
½ teaspoon salt
½ cup milk
Zest of 2 lemons
Cooking spray

Glaze and decorations:
¾ cup + 3 tablespoons unsalted
 butter
1½ tablespoons heavy cream
¼ cup + 2 tablespoons light corn
 syrup
Large pinch of salt
1½ teaspoons vanilla extract
4¾ cups confectioners' sugar
White food coloring
DIY Candy Eyes (page 91)

Bake the cakes:
1. Preheat the oven to 350°F. Place the butter in a large bowl and beat with an electric mixer until light and fluffy. Add the sugar and mix well. Add the eggs one at a time, beating well after each addition.

2. Sift together the flour, baking powder, and salt in a separate bowl. Add this to the butter mixture in 2 additions, alternating with milk (flour mixture > milk > flour mixture).

3. Add the lemon zest and fully combine.

4. Lightly spray a silicone air fryer egg mold with cooking spray. Spoon the batter into the mold, filling each cavity about ¾ of the way full. Save the remaining batter for the second batch.

5. Bake for 20 to 30 minutes, until a skewer inserted into the cakes comes out clean.

6. Allow the cakes to cool in the mold for about 10 minutes, then unmold onto a wire rack and cool completely. Make another batch with the remaining batter, making sure to grease the mold beforehand.

7. Once the cakes have cooled completely, use a serrated knife to trim off any excess cake, so that the ghosts sit upright.

Make the glaze:
1. Fill a pot with 2 to 3 inches of water and place a heatproof bowl on top. The bottom of the bowl should not be touching the water.

(Continued . . .)

2. Set it to medium-low heat and add the butter, heavy cream, and corn syrup. Stir consistently until everything has melted and combined.

3. Add the salt and vanilla extract and mix well. Gradually add the sugar until it is smooth and evenly combined. When drizzled, the glaze should stay on the surface for a second or two. Add some white food coloring until the desired shade is achieved.

Decorate:

1. Working with 2 to 3 ghosts at a time, sit the ghosts on top of upside-down shot glasses. The base of the glass should be narrower than the base of the cake. Place the glass on a rimmed baking sheet. This will catch any excess glaze.

2. Spoon the warm glaze on top of the ghosts, allowing it to evenly coat the cake. Allow the glaze to set for 1 to 2 minutes, then stick some candy eyes onto each ghost.

3. Very gently use a knife or spatula to remove excess glaze that is dripping from the base of the cakes. Then transfer the ghosts to a clean baking sheet and continue with the remaining cakes.

4. Allow the glaze to fully harden either at room temperature or in the fridge, then enjoy!

Haunted House Cake

Cake batter:

2 cups all-purpose flour
2 cups sugar
¾ cup cocoa powder
2 teaspoons baking powder
1½ teaspoons baking soda
1 teaspoon salt
1 cup milk
½ cup vegetable oil
2 large eggs
2 teaspoons vanilla extract
1 cup boiling water

Buttercream and decorations:

3 cups unsalted butter, room
   temperature
2 teaspoons vanilla extract or seeds
   from 1 vanilla bean
6½ cups confectioners' sugar
Yellow and black food coloring
1 cup chocolate chips
2 silver candles

Bake the cake:

1. Place the flour, sugar, cocoa powder, baking powder, baking soda, and salt in a large bowl and mix together.

2. Add the milk, vegetable oil, eggs, and vanilla extract and mix with an electric mixer until combined.

3. Slowly add the boiling water and mix until well combined.

4. Grease and flour three 6-inch round baking pans.

5. Divide the batter evenly between the pans and bake at 350°F for 30 to 35 minutes, until a skewer inserted into the center comes out clean. Cool for 15 minutes in the pan, then turn onto a wire rack and cool completely.

Make the buttercream:

1. Beat the butter with an electric mixer until pale and fluffy. Add the vanilla extract and confectioners' sugar 1 cup at a time, beating with each addition.

2. Dye ¾ cup of the buttercream yellow.

Assembly:

1. Stack the cakes and spread some white buttercream and half of the chocolate chips between each layer.

2. Coat the cake in a thin layer of buttercream, called a crumb coat. This will catch any excess cake crumbs. Chill the cake in the fridge for 20 minutes.

3. Dye the remaining white buttercream black. Coat the cake in a thick, generous layer of black buttercream. Smooth the surface.

(Continued . . .)

4. Divide the remaining black buttercream into 2 piping bags fitted with a small round piping tip and a large star-shaped piping tip.

5. Spread the yellow buttercream onto the sides of the cake and shape it into cathedral windows. Outline the windows using the black buttercream with the small round piping tip. Add various swirls, patterns, and decorations around the windows with the black buttercream as you please. The house should be as opulent as possible!

6. Use the black buttercream with the star-shaped piping tip to pipe dollops around the edges of the cake, as well as swirls and dollops on top.

7. Stick 2 silver candles into the dollops at the front of the cake. Right before serving, light the candles!

Trick-or-Treat Cake

Cake batter:

2 cups all-purpose flour
2 cups sugar
¾ cup cocoa powder
2 teaspoons Pumpkin Pie Spice
    (page 83)
2 teaspoons baking powder
1½ teaspoons baking soda
1 teaspoon salt
1 cup milk
½ cup vegetable oil
2 large eggs
2 teaspoons vanilla extract
1 cup boiling water

Buttercream and decorations:

3 cups unsalted butter, room
    temperature
1 teaspoon Pumpkin Pie Spice (page 83)
2 teaspoons vanilla extract or seeds
    from 1 vanilla bean
6½ cups confectioners' sugar
Orange and yellow food coloring
⅓ cup Reese's Pieces
Halloween candies

Bake the cake:

1. Place the flour, sugar, cocoa powder, Pumpkin Pie Spice, baking powder, baking soda, and salt in a large bowl and mix together.

2. Add the milk, vegetable oil, eggs, and vanilla extract and mix with an electric mixer until combined.

3. Slowly add the boiling water and mix until well combined.

4. Grease and flour three 6-inch round baking pans.

5. Divide the batter evenly between the pans and bake at 350°F for 30 to 35 minutes, until a skewer inserted into the center comes out clean. Cool for 15 minutes in the pan, then turn onto a wire rack and cool completely.

Make the buttercream:

1. Beat the butter with an electric mixer until pale and fluffy. Add the Pumpkin Pie Spice, vanilla extract and confectioners' sugar 1 cup at a time, beating with each addition.

2. Dye ¾ of the buttercream orange. Dye the remaining buttercream yellow and place it into a piping bag fitted with a large star-shaped piping tip.

Assembly:

1. Stack the cakes and spread some orange buttercream and half of the Reese's Pieces between each layer.

2. Coat the cake in a thin layer of buttercream, called a crumb coat. This will catch any excess cake crumbs. Chill the cake in the fridge for 20 minutes.

(Continued . . .)

3. Coat the cake in a thick, generous layer of orange buttercream. Smooth the surface.

4. Stick some candy on the sides of the cake. I recommend using fairly lightweight candy, as heavier candy may fall off.

5. Use the yellow buttercream to pipe a continuous swirl around the top of the cake. You can do this by holding the piping bag at a slight angle and pipe a continuous ringlet of buttercream, moving along the edge of the cake and eventually meeting the other end.

6. Stick some extra Halloween candy into the yellow buttercream. This is a great place to use heavier candy like candy pumpkins and large gummies.

3D Ghost Cake

Cake batter:

1 cup unsalted butter, room
   temperature
2 cups sugar
4 teaspoons vanilla bean paste
6 large eggs
3 cups all-purpose flour
1 teaspoon baking soda
1 teaspoon salt
1½ cups sour cream

Buttercream and decorations:

3 cups unsalted butter, room
   temperature
2 teaspoons vanilla bean paste
6½ cups confectioners' sugar
Black, pink, and orange food coloring
1 lollipop stick
1 mini Tootsie Roll

Bake the cake:

1. Beat the butter and sugar with an electric mixer until pale and smooth. Add the vanilla bean paste and eggs one at a time, mixing with each addition.

2. In a separate bowl, combine the flour, baking soda, and salt. Add this to the batter in 2 additions, alternating with the sour cream.

3. Spoon the batter into 4 greased and floured 6-inch round cake pans. Bake at 350°F for 30 minutes, or until a skewer inserted into the centers comes out clean. Cool completely.

Make the buttercream:

1. Beat the butter with an electric mixer until pale and fluffy. Add the vanilla bean paste and confectioners' sugar 1 cup at a time, beating with each addition.

2. Dye ¼ cup of the buttercream black and place it into a piping bag fitted with a small round piping tip. Dye 2 tablespoons of the buttercream pink and place it into a piping bag fitted with a medium-sized round piping tip. Dye ½ cup of the buttercream orange and set it aside.

Assembly:

1. Stack the cakes and spread some white buttercream between each layer. Use a serrated knife to cut the cake into the body of the ghost by rounding the edges at the top and curving the cake inward slightly at the sides. Reserve the cake scraps!

2. Coat the cake in a thin layer of buttercream, called a crumb coat. This will catch any excess cake crumbs. Chill the cake in the fridge for 20 minutes.

(Continued . . .)

3. Place the cake crumbs in a large bowl and add about ½ cup of buttercream. Beat with an electric mixer until the cake is broken into fine crumbs and the buttercream is evenly incorporated into the cake.

4. Use the cake crumbs to shape the ghost's arms and stick them onto the cake. Add some crumbs to the base of the cake to make it flare out a little bit. Use some more cake crumbs to create the little pumpkin, but keep this on the side, on a plate lined with plastic wrap. Place the pumpkin in the fridge while you decorate the rest of the cake.

5. Then coat the cake in a smooth, generous layer of white buttercream.

6. Draw the eyes and mouth with the black buttercream and the cheeks with the pink buttercream.

7. Place the remaining white buttercream into a piping bag fitted with a small round piping tip. Pipe sparkles into the ghost's eyes.

8. Remove the pumpkin from the fridge and place a lollipop stick into the base of the pumpkin. Then stick the pumpkin on top of the ghost, using the lollipop stick as an anchor.

9. Cover the pumpkin in orange buttercream and top with the mini Tootsie Roll.

Graveyard Pudding

12 ounces cream cheese, room
  temperature
½ cup granulated sugar
¼ cup cocoa powder
½ cup heavy cream
1 peach, finely chopped
3 Oreo cookies, finely crushed
3 gravestone cookies (from
  Gravestone Cupcakes, page 43)
Gummy worms
DIY Candy Eyes (page 91)

1. To make the cheesecake filling, beat the cream cheese, sugar, and cocoa powder with an electric mixer until smooth. Add the heavy cream and whisk until incorporated.

2. Divide half of the filling between 3 jars or bowls. Scatter the chopped peach on top, then add the rest of the filling.

3. Sprinkle the tops with crushed Oreo cookies, then stick a gravestone cookie into each bowl. Decorate with gummy worms and candy eyes.

Strawberry Ghosts

These strawberries will need to be stored in the fridge and should be consumed the same day that you make them to ensure they stay the freshest!

2 cups white chocolate, roughly chopped
1 tablespoon shortening
15 fresh strawberries, washed and dried
¼ cup dark chocolate, roughly chopped

1. Place the white chocolate in a microwave-safe bowl and microwave for 30-second intervals until melted, stirring at each interval. This will ensure that the chocolate does not burn.

2. Add the shortening to the white chocolate and mix well.

3. Line a baking sheet with parchment paper. Set aside.

4. Working with 1 strawberry at a time, dip it into the white chocolate, dipping it as far into the chocolate without touching the greens as possible. If you find that the white chocolate isn't as opaque as you'd like, allow the excess chocolate to drip off, place the strawberries on the baking sheet, chill them in the fridge for about 30 minutes, dip them again, then continue with the following step. This will coat them twice!

5. Without allowing excess chocolate to drip off, quickly transfer the strawberry to the baking sheet. Allow the chocolate to pool at the base of the strawberry. For a ghostly "tail," you can drag the strawberry upward, to encourage the chocolate to pool in a more taillike fashion.

6. Place the strawberries in the fridge until the chocolate has fully set, about 30 minutes.

7. In the meantime, place the dark chocolate in a small microwave-safe bowl. Microwave it for 30-second intervals until melted, stirring at each interval.

8. Once the strawberries have set, use a toothpick or a tiny spoon to draw faces onto the ghosts with the dark chocolate. Return the strawberries to the fridge for the dark chocolate to set and enjoy!

Gravestone Cupcakes

Marble cookie dough:

2 cups all-purpose flour
1 teaspoon ground cinnamon
¼ teaspoon salt
½ teaspoon baking powder
½ cup unsalted butter, room temperature
1 cup granulated sugar
2 tablespoons milk
1 large egg
½ teaspoon vanilla extract
Black food coloring

Cupcake batter:

1 cup all-purpose flour
1 cup sugar
¼ cup + 2 tablespoons cocoa powder
1 teaspoon baking powder
¾ teaspoon baking soda
½ teaspoon salt
½ cup milk
¼ cup vegetable oil
1 large egg
1 teaspoon vanilla extract
½ cup boiling water
1 cup Royal Icing (page 177)
Black and green food coloring

Buttercream and decorations:

2 cups unsalted butter, room
    temperature
2 tablespoons vanilla extract
½ cup milk
1½ cups cocoa powder
4 cups confectioners' sugar
10 Oreo cookies

Make the marble cookie dough:

1. Mix together the flour, cinnamon, salt, and baking powder in a bowl. In a separate bowl, cream the butter and sugar with an electric mixer until it becomes light and fluffy.

2. Add the milk, egg, and vanilla extract. Mix until well combined, then add the flour mixture and mix until just combined.

3. Shape the dough into a ball then divide into 2. Add some black food coloring to one ball and dye it black. Then swirl both balls of dough together, kneading just a couple times to create a marble effect. Wrap the dough in plastic wrap. Chill it in the fridge for 1 hour, until firm.

Bake the cupcakes:

1. Place the flour, sugar, cocoa powder, baking powder, baking soda, and salt in a large bowl and mix together.

2. Add the milk, vegetable oil, egg, and vanilla extract and mix with an electric mixer until combined.

3. Slowly add the boiling water and mix until well combined.

4. Divide the batter evenly into a lined cupcake pan and bake at 350°F for 15 to 20 minutes, until a skewer inserted into the centers comes out clean. Cool for 10 minutes in the pan, then transfer the cupcakes to a wire rack and cool completely.

Make the gravestones:

1. Preheat the oven to 350°F. Roll the marble cookie dough out on a floured surface to ¼-inch thick.

2. Use a sharp knife to cut out gravestones and place them on a baking sheet lined with parchment paper.

(Continued . . .)

3. Bake for 10 minutes, until the edges are just starting to brown. Cool completely.

4. Dye half of the Royal Icing black and place it into a piping bag fitted with a small round piping tip. Pipe "RIP" onto the cookies and allow the icing to dry completely, about 1 hour.

5. Place the remaining icing into a piping bag fitted with a small round piping tip. Pipe little bone shapes onto a baking sheet lined with parchment paper. Set aside and allow to dry, about 1 to 2 hours.

6. Dye the remaining icing green and place it in a piping bag fitted with a medium-sized round piping tip. Set aside.

Make the buttercream:

1. Beat the butter with an electric mixer until pale and fluffy.

2. Add the vanilla extract and milk and mix well. Add the cocoa powder and confectioners' sugar 1 cup at a time, beating with each addition.

Decorate:

1. Place the Oreo cookies in a Ziploc bag and crush with a rolling pin until there are both fine crumbs and larger pieces.

2. Place a generous dollop of buttercream onto each cupcake, then dunk the cupcake upside down into the cookie crumbs, coating the buttercream.

3. Turn the cupcake right side up and stick a gravestone and some bones into the buttercream. Use the green icing to pipe little tufts of grass around the gravestone.

4. Continue with the remaining cupcakes and enjoy!

Pumpkin Patch

Pumpkin Cakelettes

Cake batter:

2 large eggs
1½ cups granulated sugar
15 ounces plain pure pumpkin puree
    (not pumpkin pie filling)
½ cup unsalted butter, melted
2 tablespoons powdered instant
    coffee (optional)
2½ cups all-purpose flour
2 teaspoons baking soda
½ teaspoon salt
1½ teaspoons ground cinnamon
¾ teaspoon ground ginger
½ teaspoon ground nutmeg
⅛ teaspoon ground allspice
⅛ teaspoon ground cloves
Cooking spray

Frosting and decorations:

1 cup unsalted butter, room
    temperature
3½ cups confectioners' sugar
½ teaspoon vanilla extract
5 tablespoons plain pure pumpkin
    puree
Pinch of cinnamon
Orange food coloring
6 mini Tootsie Rolls

Bake the cakes:

1. Preheat the oven to 350°F. Whisk together the eggs, sugar, pumpkin puree, butter, and instant coffee (if using) in a large bowl.

2. In a separate bowl, mix together the flour, baking soda, salt, cinnamon, ground ginger, nutmeg, allspice, and cloves. Add this to the pumpkin mixture and mix together.

3. Spray a 12-cavity mini Bundt pan generously with cooking spray. Spoon the batter into the pan and bake for 30 minutes, until a skewer inserted into the centers of the cakes comes out clean. Allow them to cool for 15 minutes in the pan, then remove from the pan and cool completely on a cooling rack.

Make the frosting:

1. Whip together the butter, confectioners' sugar, vanilla extract, pumpkin, and cinnamon in a bowl with an electric mixer until light and fluffy.

2. Add a couple drops of orange food coloring if desired.

Assembly:

1. Use a serrated knife to trim off the bases of the cakes so that they sit flat.

2. Spread some buttercream onto the base of 1 cake and place another cake on top. This will begin to form the shape of the pumpkin.

(Continued . . .)

3. Place the cakelette on a small square of parchment paper and use that as a base to rotate the cake as you apply buttercream over its entire surface. Using a cake spatula will make this easier! If you find that the buttercream isn't cooperating, place the cake in the fridge for a couple minutes for the buttercream to stiffen.

4. Stick a mini Tootsie Roll into the middle of each pumpkin as a stem.

Pumpkin Cinnamon Rolls

Brioche:

⅓ cup whole milk, warm
2¼ teaspoons active dry yeast
5 large eggs, room temperature,
    divided
3½ cups all-purpose flour, divided
Black food coloring
⅓ cup granulated sugar
1 teaspoon salt
2 teaspoons Pumpkin Pie Spice
    (page 83)
1½ cups unsalted butter, room
    temperature and divided in half
Butter for greasing the pans

Filling:

½ cup pure pumpkin puree
2 teaspoons Pumpkin Pie Spice
    (page 83)
1 cup white chocolate chips, melted
2 ounces cream cheese, room
    temperature
2 tablespoons confectioners' sugar
Orange food coloring, *optional*

Frosting:

8 ounces cream cheese
1½ cups confectioners' sugar
3 tablespoons pure pumpkin puree
½ teaspoon vanilla extract
½ teaspoon Pumpkin Pie Spice (page 83)
Orange food coloring, *optional*

1. Pour the milk, yeast, 1 egg, and 1 cup flour into the bowl of an electric mixer. Mix to combine, then sprinkle over another 1 cup of flour. Let rise at room temperature for 40 minutes.

2. Add the remaining 4 eggs to the dough, along with a couple drops of black food coloring, sugar, salt, 1 more cup of flour, and Pumpkin Pie Spice. Place these into a mixer fitted with a dough hook attachment and mix on low speed for 2 minutes. Add the remaining ½ cup flour and mix on medium speed for 15 minutes.

3. Reduce the speed to medium-low and gradually add ¾ cup of butter. Increase the speed to medium-high and beat for 1 minute, then reduce the speed to medium and beat for 5 minutes.

4. Place the dough in a large buttered bowl and cover with plastic wrap. Let rise for 2½ hours.

5. Deflate the dough, cover again with plastic wrap, and let sit at room temperature for 4 to 6 hours, or leave it in the fridge to rise overnight.

6. Divide the dough in half and place it on a floured work surface. Roll it out to an 11 × 13-inch rectangle. Evenly disperse half of the remaining butter onto the surface of the dough, then fold the dough into thirds, like a letter.

7. Roll the dough out again into an 11 × 13-inch rectangle, then fold into thirds again. Wrap it tightly in plastic wrap and place it in the fridge for 30 minutes. Repeat with the remaining dough.

(Continued . . .)

8. Make the filling by placing the pure pumpkin puree, Pumpkin Pie Spice, melted white chocolate, cream cheese, and confectioners' sugar in a bowl and mixing until well combined. Add a couple drops of orange food coloring, if desired. Set aside.

9. Place 1 piece of dough on a floured surface and roll it out into an 11 × 13-inch rectangle. Spread half of the filling onto the dough, leaving the top quarter of the dough bare. Roll the dough into a log, starting with the end with the filling and ending with the bare end. Wrap in plastic wrap and place in the freezer for 45 minutes. Repeat with the remaining dough. (Note: if making these for a particular event, you can complete the previous steps a day in advance and start from Step 10 on the day you are serving them).

10. Grease a 9 × 11-inch baking dish with butter and set aside.

11. Unwrap the logs and slice them into 1½-inch-thick buns, making 14 buns. Place them into the baking dish, spacing them evenly apart. Let the buns rise at room temperature for 1½ hours.

12. Preheat the oven to 350°F. Bake the buns for 35 to 40 minutes, until golden brown.

13. To make the frosting, place the cream cheese in a bowl and beat with an electric mixer for 2 minutes, until the cream cheese is light and fluffy. Add the confectioners' sugar, pure pumpkin puree, vanilla extract, and Pumpkin Pie Spice and mix well. If desired, add a couple drops of orange food coloring for a more vibrant color.

14. Spread the frosting onto the buns and enjoy!

Pumpkin Spice Hot Chocolate

2 cups milk
½ cup heavy cream
7 ounces good-quality milk or dark chocolate
1 teaspoon Pumpkin Pie Spice (page 83)
¼ cup canned plain pumpkin (not pumpkin pie filling)

Topping:
2 cups heavy cream, cold
1 teaspoon vanilla extract
¼ cup confectioners' sugar
1 teaspoon Pumpkin Pie Spice (page 83)
2 candy pumpkins

1. Place the milk, cream, chocolate, Pumpkin Pie Spice, and pure pumpkin puree into a small pot and bring to a simmer.

2. Heat until the chocolate has melted and everything is well combined. Set aside.

3. To make the topping, place the heavy cream, vanilla extract, and confectioners' sugar into a large bowl. Beat with an electric mixer until soft peaks form. Add the Pumpkin Pie Spice and continue mixing until stiff peaks form. Place the cream into a piping bag fitted with a large star-shaped piping tip.

4. Pour the hot chocolate into 2 mugs and pipe a swirl of cream on top. Garnish each mug with a candy pumpkin and enjoy!

Pumpkin Hand Pies

Piecrust:

2½ cups all-purpose flour
1 teaspoon salt
1 teaspoon granulated sugar
1 cup cold unsalted butter, cut into
 cubes
¼–½ cup cold water
1 large egg, beaten

Filling:

⅔ cup graham crackers
¼ cup pure pumpkin puree
½ cup white chocolate chips, melted
1–2 teaspoons Pumpkin Pie Spice
 (page 83)
1 ounce cream cheese, room
 temperature
1 tablespoon confectioners' sugar

Make the piecrust:

1. Mix together the flour, salt, and sugar in a food processor. Add butter and pulse until it turns into a crumbly meal-like texture.

2. Transfer the mixture to a bowl and drizzle over the ice water. Mix with your hands until the dough sticks together when squished together.

3. Shape the dough into a disk and wrap it in plastic wrap. Place it in the refrigerator for 1 hour until firm.

Make the filling:

1. Place the graham crackers, pure pumpkin puree, melted white chocolate chips, Pumpkin Pie Spice, cream cheese, and confectioners' sugar in a blender and pulse until smooth.

2. Transfer the filling to a piping bag.

Assemble:

1. Preheat the oven to 400°F. Roll the dough out on a floured surface to ⅛-inch thick. Use a 3-inch pumpkin cookie cutter to cut out as many pumpkins as possible.

2. Place half of the pumpkins on a baking sheet lined with parchment paper.

3. Pipe the filling into the center of each pumpkin.

4. Wet your finger, then wet the edges of the filled pumpkins. Place an unused pumpkin on top, press the seams gently to seal them with your fingers, then use a fork to crimp the edges.

5. Brush the surfaces of the pies with the beaten egg. Use a sharp knife to cut two vertical slits into each pumpkin. This will allow air to escape while baking.

6. Bake the pies for 30 minutes, or until the crusts are golden brown.

7. Cool until warm, then enjoy!

Pumpkin Pie Hot Chocolate Melts

"Crust":

2 cups high-quality milk chocolate
3 teaspoons Pumpkin Pie Spice
   (page 83)
3 teaspoons cinnamon
1½ teaspoons ground ginger
1 teaspoon nutmeg
¼ teaspoon allspice
¼ teaspoon cloves

"Filling":

1 cup high-quality white chocolate
Orange oil-based food coloring
⅓ teaspoon cinnamon
¼ teaspoon ground ginger
⅛ teaspoon nutmeg
Pinch of allspice
Pinch of cloves

¼ cup Royal Icing (page 177)

Make the "crust":

1. Place the milk chocolate in a microwave-safe bowl and microwave for 30-second intervals until melted, stirring at each interval.

2. Add the cinnamon, ground ginger, nutmeg, allspice, and cloves, then mix well.

3. Spoon the "crust" into either silicone cupcake liners or cupcake liners that have been lined with plastic coating. This will ensure that they will peel off easily and not get stuck to the chocolate! Smooth the surface of the chocolate.

4. Place the filled liners on a tray and chill in the fridge for 30 minutes, or until fully hardened.

Make the "filling":

1. Place the white chocolate in a microwave-safe bowl and microwave for 30-second intervals until melted, stirring at each interval.

2. Add a couple drops of orange oil-based food coloring and mix well. Then add the cinnamon, ground ginger, nutmeg, allspice, and cloves, and mix until well combined.

3. Spoon some "filling" on top of each "crust," leaving a bit of space around the edge so that it looks like a piecrust. Spoon this on top slowly, so that it doesn't spread out too quickly.

4. Return the filled liners to the fridge and chill until the filling has fully hardened.

Decorate and serve:

1. Remove the pies from the cupcake liners.

2. Place the Royal Icing into a piping bag fitted with a small star-shaped piping tip. Pipe a swirly dollop onto the center of each pie. Allow the Royal Icing to fully harden, at least 30 minutes.

3. To serve, place 1 pie into a mug. Pour about 1½ to 2 cups of hot milk on top and stir until the pie has completely melted.

4. Enjoy your pumpkin spice hot chocolate!

Jack-o'-Lantern Cake

MAKES 1 (6-INCH) CAKE

The melted butterscotch chips and pumpkin pie spice in the batter make this cake taste wonderfully warm and subtly autumnal!

Cake batter:

1 cup unsalted butter, room temperature
2 cups sugar
3 teaspoons vanilla extract
6 large eggs
3 cups all-purpose flour
2 teaspoons Pumpkin Pie Spice (page 83)
1 teaspoon baking soda
1 teaspoon salt
1½ cups sour cream
1 cup melted butterscotch chips

Buttercream and decorations:

2 cups unsalted butter, room temperature
1 teaspoon vanilla extract or seeds from 1 vanilla bean
1 teaspoon Pumpkin Pie Spice (page 83)
5 cups confectioners' sugar
Orange, green, pink, black, and brown food coloring
½ cup chocolate chips

Bake the cake:

1. Beat the butter and sugar with an electric mixer until pale and smooth. Add the vanilla extract and eggs one at a time, mixing with each addition.

2. In a separate bowl, combine the flour, Pumpkin Pie Spice, baking soda, and salt. Add this to the batter in 2 additions, alternating with the sour cream. Add the melted butterscotch chips and mix until combined.

3. Spoon the batter into 3 greased and floured 6-inch round cake pans. Bake at 350°F for 30 minutes, or until a skewer inserted into the centers comes out clean. Cool completely.

Make the buttercream:

1. Beat the butter with an electric mixer until pale and fluffy. Add the vanilla extract, Pumpkin Pie Spice, and confectioners' sugar 1 cup at a time, beating with each addition.

2. Dye ¾ of the buttercream orange. Divide the remaining buttercream into 3 bowls and dye it green, pink, and black. Place both the green and pink buttercream into piping bags fitted with medium-sized round piping tips. Place the black buttercream into a piping bag fitted with a small round piping tip.

Assembly:

1. Stack the cakes and spread some orange buttercream and half of the chocolate chips between each layer.

(Continued . . .)

2. Coat the cake in a thin layer of buttercream, called a crumb coat. This will catch any excess cake crumbs. Chill the cake in the fridge for 20 minutes.

3. Coat the cake in a thick, generous layer of orange buttercream. Smooth the sides. Use a cake spatula, or the back of a spoon, to smear lines into the top of the cake to look like the ridges of a pumpkin.

4. Dye the remaining orange buttercream brown with the addition of brown food coloring. Place it into a piping bag fitted with a large round piping tip.

5. Pipe a large squiggle at the top of the cake to create the pumpkin's stem. Use the green buttercream to create the leaves, wiggling the piping tip as you pipe it downward to create the texture in the leaves.

6. With a toothpick, etch out the desired pumpkin face, then fill it in with the black buttercream. Lastly, pipe two dollops of pink buttercream onto the cheeks of the pumpkin.

Jack-o'-Lantern Stained Glass Cookies

Cookie dough:
2 cups all-purpose flour
1 teaspoon ground cinnamon
¼ teaspoon salt
½ teaspoon baking powder
½ cup unsalted butter, room
    temperature
1 cup granulated sugar
2 tablespoons milk
1 large egg
½ teaspoon vanilla extract
¼ cup orange hard candy

Icing:
1 batch Royal Icing (page 177)
Orange and brown food coloring

Bake the cookies:
1. Preheat the oven to 350°F.

2. Mix together the flour, cinnamon, salt, and baking powder in a bowl. In a separate bowl, cream the butter and sugar with an electric mixer until it becomes light and fluffy.

3. Add the milk, egg, and vanilla extract. Mix until well combined, then add the flour mixture and mix until just combined.

4. Shape the dough into a ball and wrap in plastic wrap. Chill it in the fridge for 1 hour, until firm.

5. Roll the cookie dough out on a floured surface to ¼-inch thick. Use a pumpkin-shaped cookie cutter to cut out cookies and place them on a baking sheet lined with parchment paper. Use a sharp knife to cut out eyes and mouths from the pumpkins.

6. Place the hard candy in a Ziploc bag and whack with a rolling pin until crushed. They don't need to be crushed into fine pieces, just pieces small enough to fit into the holes you cut for the eyes and mouth. Place the candy into these spaces.

7. Bake them for 10 minutes and cool completely on the baking sheet.

Decorate:
1. Dye ¾ of the Royal Icing orange. Place it into a piping bag fitted with a small round piping tip.

2. Look at the pumpkin cookie and imagine it being divided into 5 vertical segments, like a real pumpkin. Pipe outlines of alternating segments and fill them in with the orange icing. For example, start with the first, third, and fifth segments

or the second and fourth segments. Allow these to dry for 1 to 2 hours.

3. Now pipe and fill in the remaining segments. This will create the puffy, defined look that real pumpkins have! Allow this to dry for 1 hour.

4. Lastly, dye the remaining icing brown and place it into a piping bag fitted with a small round piping tip. Create the stem of the pumpkin by piping long, vertical squiggles ontc the stem section of the cookie.

5. Allow the icing to dry completely, about 6 hours. Then enjoy!

Rainbow Pumpkin Marshmallows

MAKES 5 (3-INCH) MARSHMALLOWS

Cooking spray
⅓ cup and ¼ cup cold water, divided
2½ teaspoons powdered gelatin
1 cup sugar
1 teaspoon vanilla extract (or seeds
    from 1 vanilla bean)
Pink, orange, yellow, green, and blue
    food coloring
3 mini Tootsie Rolls

Sugar coating:
¼ cup cornstarch
¼ cup confectioners' sugar

1. Generously spray a silicone pumpkin mold with cooking spray. Place on a baking sheet and set aside.

2. Pour ⅓ cup of cold water into the bowl of an electric mixer and sprinkle the powdered gelatin on top. Let sit for 5 minutes.

3. Place the sugar and ¼ cup cold water in a small pot and set to medium-high heat. Stir until the sugar has melted.

4. Attach a candy thermometer to the pot and boil the sugar until it reaches 238°F. Brush the sides of the pot with a wet pastry brush if sugar crystals stick to the sides. Remove the pot from the heat and stir until the sugar stops boiling.

5. Add the hot sugar to the gelatin and stir the mixture by hand, whisking for a few minutes to slightly cool. Then beat with an electric mixer on medium-high speed for 8 to 10 minutes, until soft peaks form. Add the vanilla bean seeds or extract and mix until combined.

6. Working quickly, divide the mixture into 5 bowls and dye it pink, orange, yellow, green, and blue. Spoon the marshmallow mixture into piping bags and snip off the ends, creating medium-sized holes.

7. Pipe the marshmallow into the pumpkin mold, creating one pumpkin per color. Leave the marshmallows to set overnight, for at least 6 hours, until bouncy and set when poked with your finger.

8. Gently unmold the pumpkins and place them on a baking sheet.

9. Unwrap the Tootsie Rolls and microwave them for 20 to 30 seconds, until malleable. Cut each Tootsie Roll in half and roll the halves into pumpkin stems, with one flat side and one pointed side. Stick the stems pointy-side down into the center of each pumpkin.

10. In a small bowl, combine the cornstarch and confectioners' sugar to create the sugar coating. Place it in a mesh sieve and dust it over all sides of the marshmallows Return the excess sugar coating to the bowl and bounce the marshmallows in the empty mesh sieve a couple times, to remove any excess powder.

11. Serve the marshmallows in a big cup of hot chocolate and enjoy!

Pumpkin Ice Cream

14 ounces heavy cream, cold
4 large eggs
5 ounces granulated sugar
1 teaspoon vanilla extract
2 teaspoons Pumpkin Pie Spice (page 83)
⅓ cup pure pumpkin puree
Orange food coloring
Mini Tootsie Rolls

1. Beat the heavy cream with an electric mixer until soft peaks form. Place in the fridge.

2. In a separate bowl, lightly whisk the eggs, then add the sugar and vanilla extract. Beat well until the mixture thickens and forms a ribbon when lifted. Add half of the cream, the Pumpkin Pie Spice, pure pumpkin puree, and a couple drops of orange food coloring. Mix together. Add the remaining cream and gently fold to combine.

3. Pour into a Tupperware container and seal with the lid. Place this in the freezer for 7 to 8 hours to chill and set.

4. To serve, use an ice cream scoop to create a little ball of ice cream. Serve it in a bowl or a cone and top with a mini Tootsie Roll to create the pumpkin's stem!

Meringue Pumpkins

4 large egg whites, room
temperature
½ teaspoon cream of tartar
Pinch of salt
1 cup granulated sugar
1 teaspoon vanilla extract
½ teaspoon Pumpkin Pie Spice (page 83)
Orange, green, and brown food
coloring
10 lollipop sticks
DIY Candy Eyes (page 91)

1. Preheat the oven to 225°F. Line 2 large cookie sheets with parchment paper and set aside.

2. Place the egg whites, cream of tartar, and salt into a large mixing bowl. Beat with an electric mixer on low speed until the eggs look foamy. The mixing bowl and the whisks must be completely clean and grease-free, as the egg whites will not whip otherwise.

3. Increase the speed to high and add the granulated sugar 1 tablespoon at a time, until all of the sugar has been added and is dissolved. You'll know that the sugar has dissolved if you rub a small amount of meringue between your fingers and do not feel any graininess. Beat until the meringue is thick and glossy and holds stiff peaks.

4. Add the vanilla extract and Pumpkin Pie Spice and gently stir to combine. Remove ¼ of the meringue from the bowl and divide that smaller amount into 2 other bowls. Dye the large amount of meringue orange with some orange food coloring and dye the smaller bowls green and brown.

5. Place the orange meringue and brown meringue into piping bags fitted with large star-shaped piping tips. Place the green meringue into a piping bag fitted with a medium-sized leaf piping tip.

6. Arrange the lollipop sticks onto the cookie sheets and use a tiny bit of meringue to hold them in place. Pipe the pumpkins directly onto the lollipop sticks. I piped 3 short lines, then a circle surrounding them to form the pumpkin shape. Pipe a little dollop of brown meringue up top to create the stem, then a couple leaves with the green meringue. Stick two candy eyes onto each pumpkin.

7. Bake them in the oven for 1 hour. Once they've finished baking, do not open the oven! Turn off the oven and keep them in the oven with the door closed for 2 hours, until they are cooled completely. They will be crisp and will easily peel up from the parchment paper.

8. Store them in an airtight container and enjoy!

Pumpkin Spice Sprinkles

MAKES ABOUT 5 CUPS OF SPRINKLES

¾ cup warm water
5 tablespoons meringue powder
1 teaspoon cream of tartar
2.2 pounds confectioners' sugar
1 teaspoon vanilla extract
6 teaspoons cinnamon
3 teaspoons ground ginger
2 teaspoons nutmeg
½ teaspoon allspice
½ teaspoon cloves
Orange and brown food coloring

1. Pour the warm water into a large bowl. Add the meringue powder and whisk for a couple seconds until frothy. Add the cream of tartar and whisk again.

2. Add the confectioners' sugar all at once and using an electric mixer, mix on low speed for 10 minutes. The icing should stay on the surface for 5 to 7 seconds when drizzled.

3. Add the vanilla extract and spices and mix well.

4. Divide the icing into 3 bowls. Leave one bowl white and dye the other bowls and orange and brown.

5. Place the icing into piping bags fitted with small round piping tips.

6. Line several large baking sheets with parchment paper. Pipe long lines of each color of icing onto the baking sheets. Leave the sprinkles at room temperature overnight, or until the icing has completely hardened and dried.

7. Use a knife to cut the long lines into sprinkles! You can make them as short or as long as you like.

8. To store, keep in an airtight container or jar.

Pumpkin Snickerdoodles

Cookie dough:

1½ cups all-purpose flour
1½ teaspoons Pumpkin Pie Spice
   (page 83)
¼ teaspoon cream of tartar
½ teaspoon baking soda
½ teaspoon salt
½ cup unsalted butter, melted and
   cooled
½ cup granulated sugar
⅓ cup brown sugar
¼ cup pure pumpkin puree, not
   pumpkin pie filling
1 large egg yolk
1 teaspoon vanilla extract

Sugar topping:

¼ cup granulated sugar
2 teaspoons ground cinnamon

1. Combine the flour, Pumpkin Pie Spice, cream of tartar, baking soda, and salt in a small bowl. Set aside.

2. In a large bowl, combine the butter and both the granulated sugar and brown sugar. Beat with an electric mixer until light, fluffy, and well combined.

3. Add the pumpkin puree, egg yolk, and vanilla extract and mix until combined.

4. Add the dry ingredients to the bowl and mix until just combined.

5. Cover the bowl with plastic wrap and chill in the fridge for about 45 minutes.

6. Preheat the oven to 350°F. Line a baking with parchment paper and set aside.

7. Combine the ingredients for the sugar topping in a small bowl. Set aside.

8. Roll the cookie dough into 1½ tablespoon-sized balls, then roll them in the sugar topping. Place them on the baking sheet about 2 inches apart.

9. Bake for 10 to 12 minutes, until the cookies have slightly spread and the top has crackled.

10. 10. Cool completely, then enjoy!

Pumpkin Cones

5 chocolate cupcakes (from
  Gravestone Cupcakes recipe,
  page 43)
½ cup white chocolate, melted
2 large chocolate waffle cones
¾ cup unsalted butter, room
  temperature

Frosting and decorations:

9 ounces cream cheese, room
  temperature
1 teaspoon vanilla extract or vanilla
  bean paste
3 cups confectioners' sugar
Orange, yellow, and green food
  coloring
2 green birthday candles

1. Crumble the cupcakes into a fine crumb in a large bowl. Add the melted white chocolate and mix well. You can use a hand mixer to easily break up the cupcakes and mix the chocolate in.

2. Gently pack the cake mixture into the waffle cones. If you're too rough, the waffle cones might break. Roll the remaining cake into 2 balls and press them on top, to create the "ice cream scoop." Place these into the fridge to stiffen for about 10 minutes. Don't chill them for too long, as it will be difficult to stick the candle into the top if the cake is too firm.

Make the frosting:

1. Beat the butter and cream cheese with an electric mixer until smooth. Add the vanilla extract and confectioners' sugar, 1 cup at a time, beating until light and fluffy. Add a couple drops of orange and yellow food coloring. The yellow will make the orange a little more vibrant.

2. Place the buttercream into a piping bag fitted with a large, round piping tip. Starting from the bottom of the cake ball, pipe stripes upwards, creating the ridges of a pumpkin.

3. Add some green food coloring to the remaining orange buttercream, to dye it green. Divide the buttercream into 2 piping bags, fitted with a medium-sized leaf piping tip and a small, round piping tip.

4. Stick a green candle into the center of each pumpkin. If you only chilled your ice cream cones for a couple minutes, the candle should stick in easily. Pipe the leaves around the candle, wiggling the bag to create texture in the leaves. Then pipe the vines and enjoy!

Pumpkin No-Bake Cheesecake

Crust:

3 tablespoons unsalted butter
5 cups marshmallows
1 teaspoon vanilla extract
Purple food coloring
5 cups crispy rice cereal
6 ounces white chocolate, melted
Cooking spray

Filling:

21 ounces cream cheese, room
   temperature
½ cup granulated sugar
2½ cup heavy cream
1 tablespoon Pumpkin Pie Spice
   (page 83)
⅓ cup pure pure pumpkin puree
2 tablespoons lemon juice
1 teaspoon vanilla extract
3¼ teaspoons powdered gelatin
¼ cup water
Orange and brown food coloring

Make the crust:

1. Place the butter and marshmallows in a large bowl and microwave for 30-second intervals, until both the butter and marshmallows have melted. Stir at each interval.

2. Add the vanilla extract and purple food coloring and mix well.

3. Add the crispy rice cereal and mix until it is evenly incorporated into the melted marshmallow.

4. Spray the inside of a 9-inch round springform pan with cooking spray. Press the cereal treat mixture into the base and sides of the pan. You can use your hands or a flat-bottomed cup to help do this, but be sure to spray them with cooking spray first so that they don't stick!

5. Place the pan in the fridge to stiffen for 20 minutes.

6. Use a spatula to evenly spread the melted white chocolate onto the bottom and sides of the crust. This will act as a barrier between the crust and the filling, preventing the crust from getting soggy. Return this to the fridge while you make the filling.

Make the filling:

1. Place the cream cheese and sugar in a large bowl and beat with an electric mixer until smooth.

2. Add the heavy cream, Pumpkin Pie Spice, pure pumpkin puree, lemon juice, and vanilla extract and mix until well combined.

(Continued . . .)

3. Combine the gelatin and the water in a small bowl and let the gelatin bloom for about 5 minutes. Then place the bowl in the microwave and heat for 30 seconds, until the gelatin is liquid. Pour this into the cheesecake mixture and mix until fully combined. Add a couple drops of orange food coloring and mix until evenly incorporated.

4. Pour the filling into the prepared crust, reserving about ¼ cup of filling. Smooth the surface. Chill the cake in the fridge for about 30 minutes, just until the surface is starting to set.

5. In the meantime, add some brown food coloring to the reserved filling.

6. Once the cake is out of the fridge, use a toothpick to gently draw an outline of the type of Jack-o'-Lantern face you'd like to have on your cheesecake. This will be a handy guide for the next step, when you fill in that outline with the brown cheesecake mixture. Use a small spoon to do this, and use the toothpick to help to bring any areas to a point.

7. Return the cheesecake to the fridge and chill for 6 hours or up to overnight, until the filling is firm.

8. Gently unlatch the sides of the pan and slide them off the cheesecake, then slice and serve!

Pumpkin Hot Chocolate Bombs

MAKES 6 BOMBS, 2 OF EACH COLOR

3 cups white candy melts
1 cup orange candy melts
5 pieces green candy melts
2 Tootsie Rolls

White chocolate ganache:
1½ cups good quality white
   chocolate, finely chopped
¼ cup heavy cream, hot
pinch of salt
1 teaspoon Pumpkin Pie Spice (page 83)

Milk chocolate ganache:
3 cups good quality milk chocolate,
   finely chopped
½ cup heavy cream, hot
2 tablespoons pure pumpkin puree
3 teaspoons Pumpkin Pie Spice
   (page 83)
1 tablespoon instant coffee powder

Make the shell:

1. Place the white and orange candy melts into 2 separate microwave-safe bowls. Microwave for 30-second intervals until melted, stirring at each interval.

2. Divide the melted white candy melts into 2 bowls. Leave one bowl white and add the 5 pieces of green candy melts to one bowl. Place that bowl back into the microwave and heat for 30-second intervals until the green candy melts have melted and it is a pale green color.

3. Spread all three colors of candy melts onto the walls of a 6-cavity pumpkin-shaped silicone mold. You should have some leftover melted candy melts in all three colors. Save these for later, as you will need this to seal them closed!

4. Place the mold in the fridge for 30 minutes to 1 hour to set.

Make the white chocolate ganache:

1. Place the white chocolate in a microwave-safe bowl. Microwave for 30-second intervals until melted, stirring at each interval.

2. Combine the melted white chocolate, cream, salt, and Pumpkin Pie Spice and mix until mostly combined.

3. Pour the ganache into the 2 cavities lined with the white candy melts. Leave about ¼ inch of space from the top of the cavity. Return the mold to the fridge while you make the other flavor of ganache.

Make the milk chocolate ganache:

1. Place the milk chocolate in a microwave-safe bowl. Microwave for 30-second intervals until melted, stirring at each interval.

2. Combine the melted milk chocolate, cream, pumpkin puree, and Pumpkin Pie Spice and mix until mostly combined. Do not add the instant coffee just yet!

3. Pour half of the ganache into the 2 cavities lined with orange candy melts. Leave about ¼ inch of space from the top of the cavity.

4. Add the instant coffee to the remaining ganache, mix well, then divide it between the 2 cavities lined with green candy melts. Leave about ¼ inch of space from the top of the cavity.

5. Place the mold back in the fridge for about 2 hours, or overnight.

Finishing touches:

1. Re-melt the white, green, and orange candy melts in individual microwave-safe bowls until melted.

2. Remove the mold from the fridge and fill the molds the remainder of the way full with the corresponding colors of candy melts.

3. Return the mold to the fridge for about 30 minutes, until the candy melts have hardened.

4. Gently unmold the pumpkins and place on your desired serving platter.

5. Unwrap the Tootsie Rolls and microwave them for 20 to 30 seconds, until malleable. Cut each Tootsie Rolls in half and roll the halves into pumpkin stems. Use some extra melted candy melts to attach them to the pumpkins. The residual cool temperature of the pumpkins should set the candy melts at room temperature, but if not, pop the pumpkins back into the fridge for about 5 minutes.

To serve:

1. Place a pumpkin in a mug. These are large pumpkins, so use a big mug!

2. Pour hot milk on top and give them a stir.

3. Enjoy!

Pumpkin Pie Spice

3 teaspoons ground cinnamon
¾ teaspoon ground nutmeg
¾ teaspoon ground ginger
Heaping ¼ teaspoon ground cloves

1. Mix all spices and enjoy!

Creepy Carnival

Haunted Chocolate Cookies

The DIY Candy Eyes in this book handle the temperature of the oven much better than store-bought candy eyes, so I definitely recommend making them as well. I found that store-bought candy eyes bubbled and melted in the oven, while my homemade recipe just slightly browned.

3 ounces unsweetened chocolate, roughly chopped
1 cup dark chocolate chips
½ cup unsalted butter
3 large eggs
1 cup + 2 tablespoons granulated sugar
Black food coloring
¾ cup all-purpose flour
⅓ teaspoon baking powder
¼ teaspoon salt
¼ cup DIY Candy Eyes (page 91)

1. Preheat the oven to 350°F. Place the unsweetened chocolate, dark chocolate chips, and butter into a pot set to medium-low heat, and stir until everything is melted.

2. Place the eggs and sugar in a bowl and whisk on high speed with an electric mixer until it forms a ribbon when lifted, about 3 minutes.

3. Add the chocolate mixture to the eggs and sugar while whisking. Add a couple drops of black food coloring and mix until incorporated.

4. Sift the flour, baking powder, and salt into the bowl and mix just until everything is combined.

5. Line a baking sheet with parchment paper and place tablespoon-sized balls of dough about 2 inches apart. Stick the candy eyes onto the cookies, then bake for 10 to 12 minutes.

6. Allow the cookies to cool for 1 minute, then transfer them to a cooling rack to cool completely.

Halloween Crispy Rice Treats

MAKES 9 SQUARES

¼ cup unsalted butter
5 cups mini marshmallows
1 teaspoon vanilla extract
5 cups crispy rice cereal
1 cup Reese's peanut butter candies
1 cup candy corn
½ cup Halloween sprinkles

1. Melt the butter in a pot over low heat. Add the mini marshmallows and mix until fully melted. Remove from the heat and add the vanilla extract.

2. Add the crispy rice cereal and mix well. Then add the candies and sprinkles and mix well.

3. Pour the mixture into 2 (8 × 8-inch) baking dishes or a 9 × 13-inch baking dish and press to flatten. You can add extra candies at this point, if desired.

4. Cool completely at room temperature, then slice and enjoy!

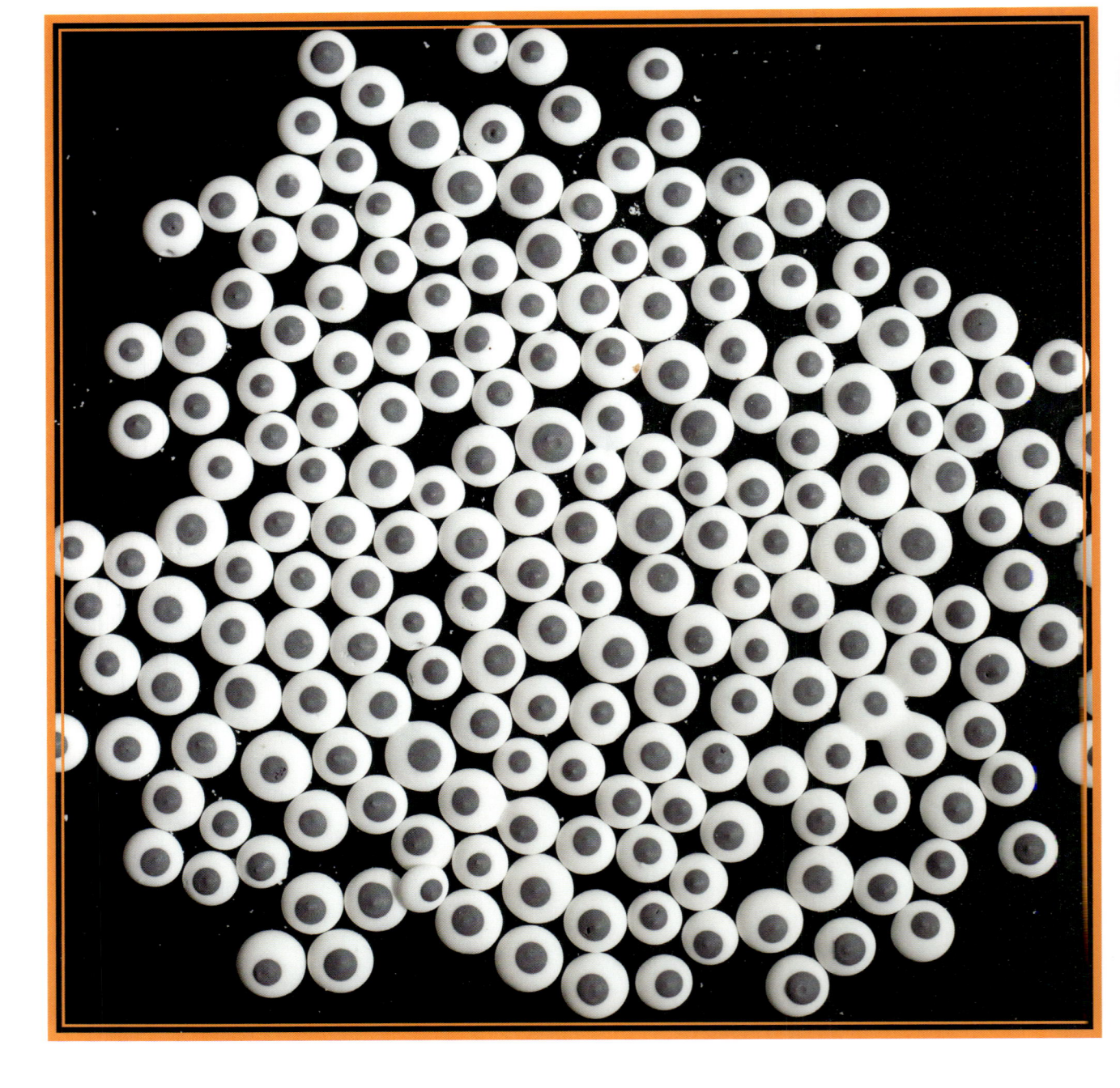

DIY Candy Eyes

MAKES ABOUT 5 CUPS OF SPRINKLES

¾ cup warm water
5 tablespoons meringue powder
1 teaspoon cream of tartar
2.2 pounds confectioners' sugar
1 teaspoon vanilla extract
Black food coloring

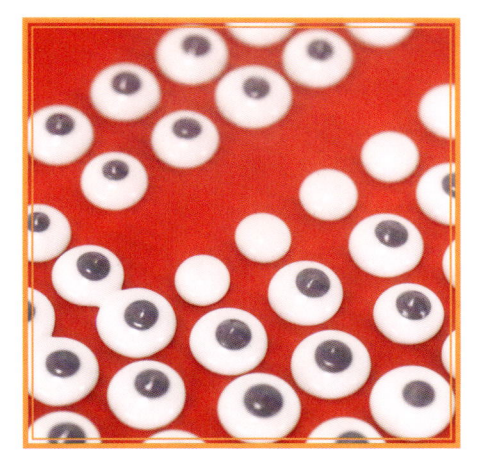

1. Pour the warm water into a large bowl. Add the meringue powder and whisk for a couple seconds until frothy. Add the cream of tartar and whisk again.

2. Add the confectioners' sugar all at once, and, using an electric mixer, mix on low speed for 10 minutes. The icing should stay on the surface for 5 to 7 seconds when drizzled.

3. Add the vanilla extract and mix well.

4. Place about ½ cup of icing into a small bowl and dye it black with the black food coloring.

5. Place the black icing into a piping bag fitted with a small round piping tip. Place the white icing into a piping bag fitted with a small/medium-sized round piping tip.

6. Line a couple baking sheets with parchment paper or silicone baking mats.

7. Pipe one row of small dollops with the white icing. Make them as large or small as you like—this will determine the size of the eyes. Once one row has been piped, pipe black dots into the center of each eye. You should do this one row at a time to prevent the white icing from drying too much before the black pupils are added.

8. Once all of the eyeballs have been piped, leave them at room temperature for at least 24 hours to dry completely. Store in a sealed container at room temperature and use as you like!

Halloween Cookie Wheel

Cookie dough:

1 cup unsalted butter, room
   temperature
½ cup granulated sugar
1 cup brown sugar
1 teaspoon salt
2 teaspoons vanilla extract
2 large eggs
2¼ cups all-purpose flour
½ teaspoon baking soda
1 cup mini marshmallows
1 cup Reese's Pieces
Cooking spray

Frosting:

9 ounces cream cheese, room
   temperature
1½ cups unsalted butter, room
   temperature
1 teaspoon vanilla extract
2½ cups confectioners' sugar
Green, green, brown, black, and red
   food coloring
Chocolate chips and chocolate
   M&M's
DIY Candy Eyes (page 91)
Green sprinkles

Bake the cookie:

1. Beat the butter, granulated sugar, and brown sugar in a bowl with an electric mixer until smooth. Add the salt, vanilla, and eggs and mix well. Add the flour and baking soda and mix until combined. Add the mini marshmallows and Reese's Pieces and mix until evenly incorporated.

2. Spray a 12-inch cookie pan (or deep-dish pizza pan) with cooking spray. Use a rubber spatula to press the cookie dough into the pan. Bake at 350°F for 15 to 20 minutes, until the edges are golden. Cool in the pan completely.

Make the frosting:

1. Beat the cream cheese and butter with an electric mixer until pale and fluffy. Add the vanilla extract and confectioners' sugar 1 cup at a time, beating until fluffy.

2. Divide the frosting into 5 bowls. Dye the frosting green, brown, black, and orange. Divide the remaining bowl of frosting in half. Dye half of that icing red and leave the remaining icing white.

3. Place the green frosting into a piping bag fitted with a large round piping tip. Place the brown frosting into a piping bag fitted with a large grass-tip piping tip. Place the black frosting into a piping bag fitted with a medium-sized angled piping tip. Place the orange frosting into a piping bag fitted with a large star-shaped piping tip. Leave the red and white frosting in its bowls.

Decorate:

1. Slice the cookie into 8 wedges, then place them back together on the serving platter of your choice. Preslicing the cookie will make serving much easier and cleaner!

(Continued . . .)

2. **Frankenstein:** Roughly pipe some green frosting onto 2 cookie wedges and use a knife to spread it evenly over the surface of the wedge. Pipe the black frosting in a back-and-forth motion to create his hair. Then transfer the black icing to another piping bag fitted with a small star-shaped piping tip. Stick 2 candy eyes onto each wedge and pipe straight eyebrows above the eyes. Stick 2 chocolate M&M's on next to the eyes as his bolts.

3. **Snake:** Starting at the top, left corner of the wedge, pipe a long, smooth swirl of green frosting, covering the entire cookie wedge. Stick 2 candy eyes onto the beginning of the swirl as its eyes. Place ⅓ of the red frosting into a piping bag fitted with a small round piping tip. Pipe the snake's tongue just below its eyes. Stick some green sprinkles onto the snake's body.

4. **Pumpkin:** This makes 2 pumpkin cookies. Starting at the widest end of the wedge, pipe lines of orange frosting downward toward the tip of the cookie. Don't overlap the ends of the frosting, as it will look a little bulky this way. Divide the remaining green frosting into 2 piping bags fitted with a small round piping tip and a medium-sized leaf piping tip. First use the round piping tip to pipe the curly vines of the pumpkin. Then use the leaf piping tip to pipe a couple of leaves where the vines begin.

5. **Ghost:** Spread the white frosting onto the entire surface of one wedge. Use the black frosting, with the star-shaped piping tip, to pipe 2 dollops for eyes and one long oval for the mouth.

6. **Werewolf:** Use a knife to spread some red frosting onto the tip of the two remaining cookies. Place the remaining white frosting into a piping bag fitted with a small round piping tip. Pipe teeth at the top of the red frosting, pointing downward toward the tip of the cookie. Use the brown frosting to pipe the werewolf's fur, piping in an upward motion to make it look as fluffy as possible. Use the same piping tip, but in a swirling motion, to pipe the werewolf's ears. Use candy eyes for its eyes and a chocolate chip for its nose.

Stuffed Skull Marshmallows

These skulls are made using large 3D skull-shaped ice cube molds. You will need to buy one mold per marshmallow, which is understandably frustrating, but they look so cool that I think it's totally worth it! This recipe can easily be halved for a smaller batch.

Cooking spray
⅓ cup + ¼ cup cold water, divided
2½ teaspoons powdered gelatin
1 cup granulated sugar
1 teaspoon vanilla extract (or seeds from 1 vanilla bean)
¼ cup raspberry jam
¼ cup cornstarch
¼ cup confectioners' sugar

1. Spray 5 silicone 3D skull molds with cooking spray. Place on a baking sheet and set aside.

2. Pour ⅓ cup of cold water into the bowl of an electric mixer and sprinkle the powdered gelatin on top. Let sit for 5 minutes.

3. Place the sugar and ¼ cup cold water in a small pot and set to medium-high heat. Stir until the sugar has melted.

4. Attach a candy thermometer to the pot and boil the sugar until it reaches 238°F. Brush the sides of the pot with a wet pastry brush if sugar crystals stick to the sides. Remove the pot from the heat and stir until the sugar stops boiling.

5. Add the hot sugar to the gelatin and stir the mixture by hand whisking for a few minutes to slightly cool. Then beat with an electric mixer on medium-high speed for 8 to 10 minutes, until soft peaks form. Add the vanilla extract and mix until combined.

6. Place the marshmallow into a piping bag and snip off the end to create a small/medium-sized hole.

7. Fill both halves of each skull mold, making sure to avoid any air bubbles in the skull faces by piping slowly. Fill back half of the skull mold completely, but leave a slight crater on the front half/face of the skull mold. Use a small spoon to fill this crater ¾ full with raspberry jam. Cover with more marshmallow, so that the mold is full, but not spilling over.

(Continued . . .)

Connect both halves of the mold and seal together. Excess marshmallow might squeeze out of the mold but that's okay! That just means that the mold is full!

8. Repeat with the remaining molds and leave them at room temperature to set for about 24 hours. These marshmallows take longer to set than usual because they are not exposed to the air and have very delicate facial features that we want to preserve!

9. Combine the cornstarch and confectioners' sugar in a bowl. Very gently unmold the marshmallows and roll them in the sugar mixture one at a time. This will coat the marshmallow and remove any stickiness, allowing them to be handled more easily.

10. These are best served the same day they are unmolded. Serve with hot chocolate and bite into them to reveal their gooey raspberry brains!

Halloween Popcorn Balls

5 tablespoons unsalted butter

1 teaspoon vanilla extract

16 ounces marshmallows

16 cups popped popcorn (about ⅔ cup unpopped kernels)

¾ cup Reese's Pieces

¾ cup candy corn and candy pumpkins

¾ cup chocolate-covered pretzels, chopped

¼ cup DIY Candy Eyes (page 91)

Cooking spray

1. Place a large sheet of parchment paper on the work surface and set it aside.

2. Melt the butter in a large pot over medium heat. Add the vanilla extract and stir to combine. Add the marshmallows and stir until fully melted.

3. Add the popcorn and mix well until it is evenly coated in the marshmallow. Turn off the heat and allow it to cool for 2 to 3 minutes. Then add half of the Reese's Pieces, candy corn, candy pumpkins, and pretzels. Mix well.

4. Spray your hands with cooking spray, then roll the popcorn into 20 balls. The cooking spray will prevent the marshmallow from sticking to your hands.

5. Press the remaining candy, as well as the candy eyes, onto the outside of the popcorn balls. You want to make sure to do this before the marshmallow stiffens.

6. Place the popcorn balls on the sheet of parchment paper and allow them to set for about 1 hour before serving.

Halloween Charcuterie Board

1 (16-inch) plastic skeleton

Cheese:
8-ounce Brie round
16 ounces orange cheddar cheese
4 ounces white cheddar cheese
8 ounces bocconcini cheese
8 ounces Havarti cheese, cut into
    cubes

Meat:
4 ounces salami
4 ounces prosciutto
7 ounces pepperoni bites

Fruit:
Blackberries
Purple grapes
Dried apricots

Extra:
Raspberry jam
White and orange cheddar cheese
    crackers
Green olives
Candy corn
Candy pumpkins
Candy eyes

Prep:

1. Use a ghost-shaped cookie cutter to cut a ghost shape out of the center of the Brie.

2. Use a pumpkin cookie cutter to cut pumpkins out of the orange cheddar cheese. Cut "BOO" out of the white cheddar with alphabet cookie cutters.

Assembly:

1. Place the plastic skeleton on the tray first and arrange it in the position you like.

2. Arrange the larger items next, like bowls for the olives and bocconcini cheese, then fill the bowls. Place candy eyes onto the bocconcini cheese. Add the Brie round. Fill the cut-out portion of the Brie with the raspberry jam. Note: you may want to place a small square of wax paper under the Brie, so that the jam doesn't soak into the tray.

3. Fill the center of the skeleton with rolled salami. Bunch the prosciutto slices into little rounds and place them in a row alongside one of the bowls.

4. Fill the remaining space with the remaining cheese, crackers, fruit, meat, and candy. Serve and enjoy!

Monster Fudge

Cooking spray
3 cups granulated sugar
¾ cup unsalted butter
⅔ cup heavy cream
1 teaspoon vanilla extract
12 ounces white chocolate
7 ounces marshmallow cream
Purple, green, and orange food
   coloring
¾ cup Halloween candy and sprinkles
DIY Candy Eyes (page 91)

1. Line an 8 × 8-inch square pan with aluminum foil and spray generously with cooking spray. Set aside.

2. Place the sugar, butter, and cream into a pot and bring to a boil over medium heat, stirring constantly. Once the mixture comes to a boil, boil for an additional 4 minutes, stirring constantly.

3. Remove from the heat and add the vanilla extract and mix well. Add the white chocolate and marshmallow cream and mix until fully combined.

4. Divide the fudge into 3 bowls—be careful, it will be hot! Dye it purple, green, and orange. Allow it to cool slightly until it begins to thicken but is still easy to pour.

5. Hold the square pan at a slight angle and pour the orange fudge into one corner of the pan. The pan will heat up as the fudge is added, so I recommend using a towel or oven mitts to hold the pan. Holding it at an angle will help the fudge stay on one side of the pan.

6. Add the green fudge next to the orange fudge, then the purple. Lay the pan flat and use a spoon or knife to swirl the colors together as you like.

7. While the fudge is still warm, decorate it with the Halloween candy and candy eyes.

8. Place the fudge in the freezer, uncovered, for about 45 minutes until fully set. Remove from the pan, peel off the foil, and slice into squares. Enjoy!

Rainbow Caramel Apples

Long lollipop sticks
6 Granny Smith apples
14 ounces caramel candies
2 tablespoons milk
2 cups white chocolate (or white candy melts), melted
1 cup each pink, orange, yellow, green, blue, and purple colored sugar

1. Stick the lollipop sticks into the top of the apples. Place them onto a baking sheet lined with parchment paper.

2. Place the caramels and milk into a pot and set to medium heat. Keep stirring until the candies have fully melted.

3. Turn off the heat and wait for the caramel to stop bubbling. Dip each apple into the caramel sauce, and fully coat it. Then place them on the baking sheet to set.

4. If any bubbles appear on the caramel, simply poke them with a sharp knife and deflate them.

5. Once the caramel has hardened, dip each apple into the melted white chocolate. Allow any excess white chocolate to drip off. There shouldn't be too much chocolate on each apple, just enough to act as "glue" for the sugar. Roll the apple into the colored sugar. You may need to roll it a couple times to get an even coating. Return the apples to the baking sheet lined with parchment paper.

6. If using white chocolate, chill the apples in the fridge for about 1 hour for the chocolate to harden. If using candy melts, let the apples sit at room temperature for about 20 minutes, until the candy melts have hardened.

7. Wrap in some cellophane bags, if desired. To serve, I've found that it's easiest to slice wedges with a sharp knife, instead of biting directly into the apple with my teeth!

Zombie Brain Crispy Rice Treats

¼ cup unsalted butter
5 cups mini marshmallows
1 teaspoon vanilla extract
2 tablespoons + ¼ cup raspberry jam, divided
Red food coloring
5 cups crispy rice cereal
Cooking spray

1. Melt the butter in a pot over low heat. Add the mini marshmallows and mix until fully melted. Remove from the heat and add the vanilla extract, 2 tablespoons raspberry jam, and red food coloring. The marshmallow should be a bright red.

2. Add the crispy rice cereal and mix well.

3. Line a baking sheet with parchment paper and spray your hands with cooking spray. Take a small handful of the cereal and shape it into a ball. Place it on the baking sheet. It may feel a little soft—this is because of the jam, but it will stiffen up as it sets! Continue with the remaining cereal.

4. Spray the handle of the butter knife with cooking spray and press it into the center of each ball, creating a brain-like shape.

5. Allow the brains to set at room temperature until firm, about 6 hours or up to overnight.

6. Before serving, brush the surface of the brains with the remaining ¼ cup raspberry jam. This will make them glisten like bloody brains!

Zombie Candy Apples

These are my favorite treats to make every year because the combination of chewy caramel and sweet chocolate is absolutely delicious! For easy eating, simply use a sharp knife to slice the apples into wedges.

Long lollipop sticks
6 Granny Smith apples
14 ounces caramel candies
2 tablespoons milk
2 cups green candy melts, melted
  (or white chocolate dyed with oil-
  based green food coloring)
½ cup black sprinkles
12 unmelted white candy melts
1 cup red candy melts, melted
½ cup dark chocolate, melted

1. Stick the lollipop sticks into the top of the apples. Place them onto a baking sheet lined with parchment paper.

2. Place the caramels and milk into a pot and set to medium heat. Keep stirring until the candies have fully melted.

3. Turn off the heat and wait for the caramel to stop bubbling. Dip each apple into the caramel sauce, and fully coat it. Then place them on the baking sheet to set.

4. If any bubbles appear on the caramel, simply poke them with a sharp knife and deflate them.

5. Once the caramel has hardened, dip each apple into the melted green candy melts (or chocolate). Allow any excess chocolate to drip off. There shouldn't be too much chocolate on each apple, just enough to evenly coat the surface.

6. Sit the apple into a bowl containing the black sprinkles, so that just the base of the apple is dipped in sprinkles. Return the apple to the baking sheet and repeat with the other apples.

7. Stick the unmelted white candy melts onto the apples as the eyes. You may need to hold them in place for a couple of seconds for them to stick without sliding off the apple.

8. Place the red candy melts into a piping bag fitted with a small/medium-sized piping tip. Starting at the lollipop stick, pipe lines outward toward the face, to look like dripping blood. Leave a little room for the candy melts to drip down. Use a toothpick to add some veins to the eyeballs. Place the apples in the fridge to chill for about 20 minutes. The cool surface will help the dark chocolate set in the next step.

9. Lastly, place the dark chocolate into a piping bag fitted with a small round piping tip. Pipe the pupils and mouth onto the apples, then return them to the fridge for the dark chocolate to set, about 30 minutes.

10. Serve and enjoy!

Pumpkin Spice Doughnuts

Doughnuts:
Cooking spray
1 large egg
¾ cups sugar
7.5 ounces plain pumpkin puree
¼ cup unsalted butter, melted
1¼ cups all-purpose flour
1 teaspoon baking soda
¼ teaspoon salt
¾ teaspoon cinnamon
¼ teaspoon ground ginger
¼ teaspoon nutmeg
Pinch allspice
Pinch cloves

Glaze:
¼ cup heavy cream
1 teaspoon vanilla extract
1 cup confectioners' sugar
¼ recipe Pumpkin Spice Sprinkles
   (page 71)

Make the doughnuts:

1. Generously spray a doughnut pan with cooking spray.

2. Combine the egg, sugar, pumpkin puree, and butter in a large bowl. In a separate bowl, combine the flour, baking soda, salt, cinnamon, ginger, nutmeg, allspice, and cloves. Add this to the pumpkin mixture and mix well.

3. Spoon the batter into a piping bag and snip off the end to create a large round tip. Pipe the batter into the doughnut pan.

4. Bake the doughnuts for 15 to 20 minutes at 350°F, until a skewer inserted into the doughnuts comes out clean.

5. Cool for 10 minutes in the pan, then flip onto a wire rack and cool completely.

Make the glaze:

1. Whisk together the heavy cream, and vanilla extract in a bowl. Add the confectioners' sugar and mix well. The glaze should be thick enough to coat the doughnuts and be opaque, but thin enough that any swirls or ripples in the glaze smooth out when you give the doughnut a little jiggle.

2. Dunk the doughnuts into the glaze and return them to the wire rack. Sprinkle with the Pumpkin Spice Sprinkles before the glaze dries and enjoy!

Halloween Bark

¼ cup pretzels, crushed
1 pound semisweet chocolate, melted
⅓ cup candy corn and candy pumpkins
2 tablespoons DIY Candy Eyes (page 91)
¼ cup Halloween sprinkles

1. Line a large baking sheet with parchment paper. Sprinkle the pretzels evenly onto the paper.

2. Pour the melted chocolate onto the pretzels and jiggle the baking sheet to spread out the chocolate and smooth the surface. The chocolate should completely cover the pretzels.

3. Sprinkle the candy corn, candy pumpkins, candy eyes, and sprinkles on top.

4. Place the baking sheet in the fridge for about 30 minutes, or until the chocolate is completely firm.

5. Break it into pieces and serve immediately.

Note: You can also temper the chocolate before using it for this bark! This will make the chocolate set at room temperature. It will have a shiny surface and will be much easier to handle.

Halloween Cookie Cake

Cookie dough:

1 cup unsalted butter, room
    temperature
½ cup granulated sugar
1 cup brown sugar
1 teaspoon salt
2 teaspoons vanilla extract
2 large eggs
2¼ cups all-purpose flour
½ teaspoon baking soda
2 cups chocolate chips
Cooking spray

Frosting and decorations:

9 ounces cream cheese, room
    temperature
1½ cups unsalted butter, room
    temperature
1 teaspoon vanilla extract
2½ cups confectioners' sugar
Orange, purple, and black food
    coloring
Halloween candy

Bake the cookie:

1. Beat the butter, granulated sugar, and brown sugar in a bowl with an electric mixer until smooth. Add the salt, vanilla, and eggs and mix well. Add the flour and baking soda and mix until combined. Add the chocolate chips and mix until evenly incorporated.

2. Spray a 12-inch cookie pan (or deep-dish pizza pan) with cooking spray. Use a rubber spatula to press the cookie dough into the pan. Bake at 350°F for 15 to 20 minutes, until the edges are golden. Cool in the pan completely.

Make the frosting:

1. Beat the cream cheese and butter with an electric mixer until pale and fluffy. Add the vanilla extract and confectioners' sugar 1 cup at a time, beating until fluffy.

2. Divide the frosting in half. Dye one half orange and one half purple. Take ⅓ of the purple frosting and add some black food coloring to dye it black.

3. Place the orange and purple frosting into piping bags fitted with large star-shaped piping tips. Place the black frosting into a piping bag fitted with a small round piping tip.

Decorate:

1. Using the black frosting, pipe a spiderweb onto the entire surface of the cookie.

2. Pipe alternating dollops of orange and purple frosting around the edges of the cookie.

3. Stick the Halloween candy onto the frosting border, and if desired, onto the cobweb.

4. Slice and enjoy!

Zombie Cake

Cake batter:

2 cups all-purpose flour
2 cups sugar
¾ cup cocoa powder
2 teaspoons baking powder
1½ teaspoons baking soda
1 teaspoon salt
1 cup milk
½ cup vegetable oil
2 large eggs
2 teaspoons vanilla extract
1 cup boiling water
Cooking spray

Cream cheese frosting and decorations:

24 ounces cream cheese, room
    temperature
1½ cups unsalted butter, room
    temperature
2 teaspoons vanilla extract
9 cups confectioners' sugar
Green, brown, black, and red food
    coloring
8 fresh strawberries, finely chopped
½ cup mini marshmallows
¼ cup mini chocolate chips
2 large marshmallows

2 toothpicks

Bake the cake:

1. Preheat the oven to 350°F. Place the flour, sugar, cocoa powder, baking powder, baking soda, and salt in a large bowl and mix together.

2. Add the milk, vegetable oil, eggs, and vanilla extract and mix with an electric mixer until combined.

3. Slowly add the boiling water and mix until well combined.

4. Grease and flour three 6-inch round baking pans.

5. Divide the batter evenly between the pans and bake for 35 to 40 minutes, until a skewer inserted into the center comes out clean. Cool for 15 minutes in the pan, then turn onto a wire rack and cool completely.

Make the frosting:

1. Place the cream cheese and butter in a large bowl and beat with an electric mixer until pale and fluffy. Add the vanilla extract and mix to combine.

2. Add the confectioners' sugar 1 cup at a time, mixing with each addition. Then beat for another 3 minutes, until light and fluffy.

Assembly:

1. Slice the tops and bottoms off the cakes to smooth the surface and remove any excess browning.

2. Stack the cakes and spread ½ cup of frosting between each layer. Scatter half of the strawberries, mini marshmallows, and mini chocolate chips onto each layer of frosting.

(Continued . . .)

3. Coat the cake in a thin layer of frosting, called a crumb coat. This will catch any excess cake crumbs. Chill the cake in the fridge for 20 minutes.

Decorate:

1. Dye ¾ of the remaining frosting green. To get a muddy, mossy green, you can add a drop or two of brown or black food coloring to the green! Divide the remaining frosting in half. Dye one half red. Leave the remaining half white for now.

2. Carve a crater out of one side of the cake. This is where the brain will go! Then coat the entire cake, including the inside of the crater, with green frosting. Stick two large marshmallows into the crater and attach to the cake with toothpicks. This will give the brain some height—just be careful when eating!

3. Place the red frosting into a piping bag fitted with a large round piping tip. Pipe rows of large squiggles onto the brain.

4. Take a piece of clean, crumpled paper towel, very lightly dip it into the remaining red frosting, and dab it all over the cake. This will create the zombie's wounds.

5. Use a knife to spread the white frosting into a circle on the cake, creating the zombie's eye. Use some extra red buttercream to create veins in the eye. This can be done by dipping a toothpick into the red frosting, then wiggling it on the eye, which will create skinny, narrow veins. For larger veins, simply transfer the red frosting to a piping bag fitted with a small round piping tip and pipe veins onto the eyes.

6. Dye the remaining white frosting black and place it in a piping bag fitted with a round, medium-sized piping tip. Pipe on the zombie's pupil, X as the other eye, and the mouth.

7. Serve and enjoy!

Witch's Coven

Cauldron Brownies

Brownies:

Cooking spray
½ cup + 2 tablespoons unsalted
    butter, melted
1 cup granulated sugar
⅔ cup cocoa powder
2 teaspoons vanilla extract
¾ teaspoon salt
2 large eggs
½ cup all-purpose flour
½ cup dark chocolate, roughly
    chopped

Filling and decorations:

1 cup unsalted butter, room
    temperature
1 teaspoon vanilla extract
3 cups confectioners' sugar
Orange, green, and purple food
    coloring
Orange, green, and purple sprinkles
24 pretzel sticks

Bake the brownies:

1. Preheat the oven to 350°F. Generously spray a 24-cup mini cupcake pan with cooking spray.

2. In a large bowl, combine the butter, sugar, cocoa powder, vanilla extract, and salt. Add the eggs and mix until combined.

3. Add the flour and dark chocolate and mix until just combined.

4. Scoop the batter into the cupcake pan and bake for 12 to 15 minutes, until the surface of the brownies is beginning to crack.

5. Once out of the oven, use a spoon to press an indentation into the center of each brownie. This will create a little crater in the centers to hold the filling and make them look more like cauldrons.

6. Allow them to cool completely in the pan, then unmold and set aside.

Make the filling:

1. Place the butter in a bowl and beat with an electric mixer until pale and fluffy. Add the vanilla extract and mix until combined.

2. Add the confectioners' sugar 1 cup at a time, beating with each addition. Then beat for 2 to 3 minutes longer, until it is pale and fluffy.

3. Divide the frosting into 3 bowls. Dye it orange, green, and purple.

Decorate:

1. Place a dollop of frosting into the middle of each brownie. Stick matching sprinkles onto the frosting, to look like a bubbling potion.

2. Stick a pretzel stick into each cauldron to look like a large spoon.

3. Serve and enjoy!

Black Cat Cookies

Cookie dough:
2 cups all-purpose flour
¼ teaspoon salt
½ teaspoon baking powder
½ cup unsalted butter, room
   temperature
1 cup granulated sugar
2 tablespoons milk
1 large egg
½ teaspoon vanilla extract

Decorations:
1 batch Royal Icing (page 177)
Black, pink, green, and orange food
   coloring
2 cups black sprinkles

Bake the cookies:
1. Preheat the oven to 350°F.

2. Mix together the flour, salt, and baking powder in a bowl. In a separate bowl, cream the butter and sugar with an electric mixer until it becomes light and fluffy.

3. Add the milk, egg, vanilla extract, and a couple drops of black food coloring. Mix until well combined, then add the flour mixture and mix until just combined.

4. Shape the dough into a ball and wrap in plastic wrap. Ch ll it in the fridge for 1 hour, until firm.

5. Roll the cookie dough out on a floured surface to ¼-inch thick. Use cat-shaped cookie cutters to cut out cookies and place them on a baking sheet lined with parchment paper.

6. Bake them for 10 minutes, then transfer to a wire rack and cool completely.

Decorate:
1. Dye ¾ of the Royal Icing black. Working with one cookie at a time, spread some black icing onto the entire surface of the cookie, then dunk the cookie into the black sprinkles, cover ng all of the icing. Repeat with the remaining cookies.

2. Divide the remaining icing into 3 bowls. Dye it pink, green, and orange and place the icing into piping bags fitted with small round piping tips.

3. Use the pink icing for the noses and the green and orange icing for the eyes and collars.

4. Allow the icing to dry at room temperature for at least 12 hours, then enjoy!

Witch Noses

These would be such a cute Halloween party favor—wrap them in cellophane and watch everyone's reactions as they realize what they are! If you're not a fan of candy melts, you can use white chocolate and dye it green with oil-based food coloring.

18 vanilla caramel squares
3 long lollipop sticks
1½ cups melted green candy melts
2 tablespoons cocoa powder

1. Unwrap 6 vanilla caramels and place them on a microwave-safe dish. Microwave them for 20 to 30 seconds, until warm and malleable.

2. Smoosh 5 of the caramels together and create the base shape of the nose. Use the remaining caramel to create the nostrils and the wart. Stick these onto the nose. If they're not sticking well, you can use a very small amount of water as "glue" to stick them together.

3. Allow the nose to cool and set while you create two more noses.

4. When the noses have set, stick a lollipop stick into the base of the noses.

5. Dunk the noses into the melted candy melts and tap the stick on the side of the bowl a couple times to remove any excess chocolate.

6. Stick the lollipop sticks into a jar of sugar or rice so that they stay upright, then place in the fridge for the chocolate to set, about 30 minutes.

7. Use a clean, food-safe paintbrush to brush cocoa powder onto the noses, creating some shadows and definition.

8. Serve and enjoy!

Chocolate Rats

MAKES 8 (4-INCH) RATS

2½ cups melted dark chocolate
Black oil-based food coloring

Filling:
3 cups good-quality dark or milk
chocolate, finely chopped
½ cup heavy cream, hot
Pinch of salt
2 tablespoons red candy melts,
melted
1 tablespoon white candy melts,
melted

1. Combine the dark chocolate and a couple drops of black oil-based food coloring. This is optional, but will make the rats look black!

2. Spread the chocolate onto the inside of an 8-cavity rat-shaped silicone mold, creating a chocolate shell. Place the mold in the fridge while you make the filling.

3. To make the filling, place the finely chopped chocolate in a bowl and pour the hot heavy cream on top. Allow to sit for 5 minutes, then add the salt and stir until fully combined.

4. Spoon the filling into the rats, leaving about ⅛ inch of space. This is important! Return the mold to the fridge for the filling to semi-set, about 20 minutes.

5. Fill the molds the remainder of the way with more melted dark chocolate. This will seal the filling into the rats and prevent it from leaking out. This will also create a solid chocolate base so that the rats can sit upright.

6. Return the mold to the fridge to finish setting, about 1 hour.

7. Unmold the rats. Place two dollops of red candy melts onto the rats as their eyes. Then use a toothpick to draw the rats' pupils with leftover dark chocolate, and their whiskers and eye sparkle with the melted white candy melts.

8. Return the rats to the fridge for these features to harden, then enjoy!

9. To serve, place a rat in a pot and add 2 cups of milk. Bring the heat up to medium and melt the rat!

Witch Hat Cupcakes

MAKES 12 CUPCAKES

Cupcake batter:

1 cup all-purpose flour
1 cup sugar
¼ cup + 2 tablespoons cocoa powder
1 teaspoon baking powder
¾ teaspoon baking soda
½ teaspoon salt
½ cup milk
¼ cup vegetable oil
1 large egg
1 teaspoon vanilla extract
½ cup boiling water

Buttercream:

2 cups unsalted butter, room
   temperature
1 teaspoon vanilla extract or seeds
   from 1 vanilla bean
5 cups confectioners' sugar
Yellow, orange, green, and purple
   food coloring
2 cups marshmallow fluff

Witch hats:

1 cup black sanding sugar
12 Oreo cookies
2½ cups chocolate chips, melted
12 mini ice cream cones
Sour belt candy

Bake the cupcakes:

1. Place the flour, sugar, cocoa powder, baking powder, baking soda, and salt in a large bowl and mix together.

2. Add the milk, vegetable oil, egg, and vanilla extract and mix with an electric mixer until combined.

3. Slowly add the boiling water and mix until well combined.

4. Divide the batter evenly between two cupcake pans and bake at 350°F for 15 to 20 minutes, until a skewer inserted into the centers comes out clean. Cool for 10 minutes in the pan then transfer the cupcakes to a wire rack and cool completely.

Make the buttercream:

1. Beat the butter with an electric mixer until pale and fluffy. Add the vanilla extract and confectioners' sugar 1 cup at a time, beating with each addition.

2. Dye about ¼ cup of the buttercream yellow with the yellow food coloring. Place the yellow buttercream into a piping bag fitted with a small round piping tip.

3. Divide the remaining buttercream into 3 bowls. Dye the buttercream orange, green, and purple and place it into piping bags fitted with large star-shaped piping tips.

Make the hats:

1. Pour the black sanding sugar into a large shallow bowl or onto a baking sheet. Lay the Oreo cookies flat on a plate. Set aside.

2. Make one hat at a time by dipping the top of one Oreo cookie in the melted chocolate chips, so that the entire top surface of the cookie is covered. Return the cookie to the plate, chocolate-side up.

(Continued . . .)

3. Pick up one ice cream cone, holding it by placing two fingers inside the cone—this is so the sides don't get crushed! Roll the sides of the cone in the melted chocolate, allowing any excess chocolate to drip off. If there is too much chocolate on the cone, the sugar will have trouble sticking.

4. Immediately roll the cone in the sanding sugar, making sure that it is evenly coated. Place the cone on top of the chocolate-dipped cookie. Sprinkle some more sanding sugar on top of the cookie so that any excess chocolate is covered in sugar. Wrap a sour belt around the base of the cone, using some extra chocolate to seal it closed. Set the hat aside on a tray and repeat to make the remaining 11 hats.

5. Chill the hats in the fridge for about 20 minutes, or until the chocolate has hardened.

6. Use the yellow buttercream to pipe a buckle onto each hat. Set aside.

Decorate the cupcakes:

1. Use a small spoon to remove the center of each cupcake. Spoon some marshmallow fluff into each cupcake. You can place the marshmallow fluff into a piping bag to make this process much easier!

2. Pipe a swirl of purple, green, or orange buttercream onto the cupcakes. Top with a hat and enjoy!

Witch's Birthday Cake

Cake batter:
2 cups all-purpose flour
2 cups sugar
¾ cup cocoa powder
2 teaspoons baking powder
1½ teaspoons baking soda
1 teaspoon salt
1 cup milk
½ cup vegetable oil
2 large eggs
2 teaspoons vanilla extract
1 cup boiling water

Buttercream and decorations:
3 cups unsalted butter, room
  temperature
2 teaspoons vanilla extract or seeds
  from 1 vanilla bean
6½ cups confectioners' sugar
Purple, orange, and black food
  coloring
Halloween candies

Bake the cake:
1. Place the flour, sugar, cocoa powder, baking powder, baking soda, and salt in a large bowl and mix together.

2. Add the milk, vegetable oil, eggs, and vanilla extract and mix with an electric mixer until combined.

3. Slowly add the boiling water and mix until well combined.

4. Grease and flour four 6-inch round baking pans.

5. Divide the batter evenly between the pans and bake at 350°F for 30 to 35 minutes, until a skewer inserted into the center comes out clean. Cool for 15 minutes in the pan, then turn onto a wire rack and cool completely.

Make the buttercream:
1. Beat the butter with an electric mixer until pale and fluffy. Add the vanilla extract and confectioners' sugar 1 cup at a time, beating with each addition.

2. Dye half of the buttercream pale purple. Divide the remaining buttercream in half. Dye one half orange and one half black.

Assembly:
1. Stack the cakes and spread some purple buttercream between each layer.

2. Coat the cake in a thin layer of buttercream, called a crumb coat. This will catch any excess cake crumbs. Chill the cake in the fridge for 20 minutes.

3. Coat the cake in a thick, generous layer of buttercream. Smooth the surface.

(Continued . . .)

4. Add a couple drops of extra purple food coloring to the remaining purple buttercream, making it a deeper purple. Place it into a piping bag fitted with a large round piping tip.

5. Divide the orange frosting into two piping bags, fitted with a medium-sized angled piping tip and a medium-sized star-shape piping tip. Do the same to the black buttercream.

Decorate:

1. Using the purple buttercream, pipe a row of dollops around the base of the cake. Pipe a row of orange dolloos, then a row of black dollops directly above.

2. Use the black buttercream with the angled tip to pipe garland around the cake. If you need a guide for the garlanc, a handy trick is to very gently press the bottom half of a round cookie cutter onto the cake, to create a U-shaped indertaticn. Do this around the entire circumference of the cake before piping the garland.

3. Pipe an orange garland directly above the black garland using the orange buttercream with the angled tip.

4. Pipe a circle of black frosting on the top of the cake and smooth it with a knife. Pipe a ring of purple dollops around the perimeter of the circle. Pipe a ring of orange, then a ring of black buttercream using the star-shaped piping tips around the perimeter of the purple ring.

5. Transfer the remaining purple buttercream to a piping bag fitted with a large star-shaped piping tip. At the highes: points of the garland, pipe a dollop of purple.

6. Decorate the cake with the Halloween candies and serve!

Black Cat Hot Chocolate Bombs

If you can't get your hands on oil-based food coloring, you can substitute the dark or milk chocolate for black candy melts! They are easier to handle as well, as they have a higher melting point and won't melt in your hands as easily. To serve, place each hot chocolate bomb in a mug and top with 1 to 2 cups of hot milk.

12 ounces high-quality dark or milk chocolate

Black oil-based food coloring

3 tablespoons cocoa powder

6 tablespoons granulated sugar

3 tablespoons mini marshmallows

1 tablespoon green candy melts, melted

1 tablespoon white candy melts, melted

1 tablespoon pink candy melts, melted

Make the shells:

1. Break the chocolate into small pieces and place it in a microwave-safe bowl. Microwave it for 20- to 30-second intervals, mixing at each interval. The chocolate can also be melted using a double boiler. Add a couple drops of black oil-based food coloring to dye the chocolate black.

2. Fill a hot chocolate bomb mold ¾ of the way full with the chocolate and gently rotate it so that the chocolate coats all sides. Place a sheet of parchment paper onto the work surface. Turn the mold upside down and allow the excess chocolate to drip onto the parchment paper. Scrape the chocolate off the parchment paper and return it to the bowl.

3. Use the flat back of a butter knife to smooth the edges of the chocolate mold. Place the mold in the fridge for 20 to 30 minutes, until the chocolate has fully set.

4. Repeat steps 2 and 3 to create a second layer of chocolate. This will prevent the chocolate shell from breaking during unmolding and assembly. When smoothing the edges of the chocolate mold with the butter knife, ensure that the edges of the shell are 1 to 3 millimeters thick. This will allow both halves to securely stick together in the following steps.

5. Gently unmold the chocolate shells and rest them on a plate or on top of small glasses, which will support the spherical shape very well and keep it from wobbling away.

(Continued . . .)

6. Pour some boiling water into a bowl and place a plate on top. The heat of the boiling water will heat up the plate. Once the plate feels warm to the touch, place once shell at a time onto the plate, curved-side up. Allow the edges of the shell to melt very slightly, then ift off the plate. This will create a flat edge on the shells and will make assembly *much* easier. Set this contraption aside, as you will need it again to assemble.

7. Pour the remaining chocolate onto a baking sheet lined with parchment paper. Place it in the fridge until it is partially set, about 10 to 20 minutes. Use a toothpick to draw triangles into the chocolate, making them slightly larger than you'd like. It helps to do this with semi-set chocolate because you'll be able to draw shapes in the chocolate without it bleeding back together and smudging the lines. Return this to the fridge to chill until completely set. You can also place this in the freezer!

Make the filling:
1. Combine the cocoa powder, sugar, and marshmallows in a small bowl.

Assembly:
1. Spoon some of the mix into one chocolate shell. You don't have to use all of the mixture. Add some marshmallows and sprinkles, if desired.

2. Take an empty shell and place it back on the heated plate and bowl from step 6. Allow it to just start to the melt the edges of the shell, then place it onto the filled shell. This will melt the edges of the shell to create a "glue" to seal both sides together!

3. Run your finger along the seam to remove any excess chocolate and seal the two shells together.

4. Set aside and continue with the remaining shells.

5. Remove the chocolate triangles from the fridge. Take one triangle at a time and gently press the edges of the triangle onto that same warm plate to smooth the edges. Use the residual melted chocolate on the edges of the triangle as glue to attach two triangles to each bomb, creating the cat's ears.

6. Use a toothpick to draw the cat's eyes with the green chocolate, the whiskers with the white chocolate and the nose with the pink chocolate.

7. Place the bombs in the fridge for the chocolate to set completely, then enjoy!

Spooky Sky Cake

Cake batter:

2 cups all-purpose flour
2 cups sugar
¾ cup cocoa powder
2 teaspoons baking powder
1½ teaspoons baking soda
1 teaspoon salt
1 cup coconut milk
½ cup vegetable oil
2 large eggs
2 teaspoons vanilla extract
1 cup boiling water
1 cup frozen raspberries, thawed and
   drained

Buttercream and decorations:

2 cups unsalted butter, room
   temperature
2 teaspoons vanilla extract or seeds
   from 1 vanilla bean
5 cups confectioners' sugar
Purple, black, and yellow food
   coloring
½ cup fresh raspberries
½ cup fresh blackberries
Yellow star sprinkles
Gold sugar sprinkles

Bake the cake:

1. Place the flour, sugar, cocoa powder, baking powder, baking soda, and salt in a large bowl and mix together.

2. Add the coconut milk, vegetable oil, eggs, and vanilla extract and mix with an electric mixer until combined.

3. Place the raspberries in a food processor and pulse until very smooth. Add this to the batter, along with the boiling water, and mix until well combined.

4. Grease and flour three 6-inch round baking pans.

5. Divide the batter evenly between the pans and bake at 350°F for 30 to 35 minutes, until a skewer inserted into the center comes out clean. Cool for 15 minutes in the pan, then turn onto a wire rack and cool completely.

Make the buttercream:

1. Beat the butter with an electric mixer until pale and fluffy. Add the vanilla extract and confectioners' sugar 1 cup at a time, beating with each addition.

2. Dye ¾ of the buttercream a deep shade of purple. Divide the remaining buttercream into thirds. Dye one bowl black and one bowl yellow and leave the remaining bowl white. Place the black buttercream into a piping bag fitted with a small round piping tip.

Assembly:

1. Stack the cakes and spread some purple buttercream and half of the fresh raspberries and blackberries between each layer.

(Continued . . .)

2. Coat the cake in a thin layer of buttercream, called a crumb coat. This will catch any excess cake crumbs. Chill the cake in the fridge for 20 minutes.

3. Coat the cake in a thick, generous layer of purple buttercream. Smooth the surface.

4. Place the white buttercream on a cake spatula (aka a palette knife) and spread it onto the top of the cake in a scalloped pattern. Don't worry about it mixing a little with the purple frosting—this is okay and will make it look like clouds!

5. Place a dollop of yellow buttercream in the "sky" area and smooth it to create a circle.

6. Use the black buttercream to draw a witch on a broomstick.

7. Decorate the sky with star and golden sugar sprinkles.

Black Cat Macarons

Macarons:

1 cup confectioners' sugar
¾ cup almond flour (not almond
  meal)
2 large egg whites
Pinch of cream of tartar
¼ cup superfine sugar
Black gel food coloring

Dark chocolate ganache and decorations:

8 ounces dark chocolate, melted
Pinch of salt
¾ cup heavy cream, hot
Raspberry jam
Black and red edible ink pens

Make the macarons:

1. Combine the confectioners' sugar and almond flour in a bowl, then sift 3 times.

2. Place the egg whites in a large bowl and beat with an electric mixer until foamy. Add the cream of tartar, then beat until soft peaks form. Add the superfine sugar and beat on high speed until stiff peaks form. Sift the dry mixture into the egg mixture and gently fold to combine.

3. Add the black gel food coloring and stir to combine.

4. Place the batter in a piping bag fitted with large round tip and pipe 1-inch rounds on baking sheets lined with parchment paper. Transfer the remaining batter to a piping bag fitted with a small round piping tip and pipe ears onto the cats. Wet your finger with water and smooth the top of the macarons. Tap the baking sheets on the countertop a couple times to remove any air bubbles. Let the macarons sit at room temperature for 30 minutes.

5. Set the oven to 375°F, heat for 5 minutes, then reduce the heat to 325°F. Bake the macarons, one sheet at a time, for 6 to 8 minutes, rotating halfway through. After each batch, increase the heat to 375°F, heat for 5 minutes, then reduce to 325°F and pop the next sheet into the oven!

6. Allow the macarons to cool on the sheet for 2 to 3 minutes, then transfer to a wire rack to fully cool.

Make the ganache:

1. Combine the melted dark chocolate, salt, and heavy cream in a bowl. Place in the fridge until the ganache has cooled and thickened.

2. Beat the ganache with an electric mixer until it slightly lightens in color and becomes creamy and a whipped consistency.

3. Place in a piping bag fitted with a round tip.

To assemble:

1. Flip the macarons over and pipe some ganache around the border of half the macarons. Dollop some raspberry jam in the center, then place another macaron on top.

2. Use the black edible ink pen to draw the cat's eyes and whiskers. Use the red pen to draw the cat's nose. Press down gently as macaron shells are delicate! Enjoy!

Eyeballs and Cookies

Lace cookies:

1 cup unsalted butter
2¼ cups brown sugar
2¼ cups rolled oats
1 teaspoon vanilla extract
1 large egg
Black food coloring
1 teaspoon salt
3 teaspoons all-purpose flour

Dip:

8 ounces cream cheese, room
    temperature
1 cup confectioners' sugar
½ teaspoon vanilla extract
½ cup heavy cream
7 fresh strawberries, finely chopped
¼ cup chocolate chips
2 tablespoons raspberry jam
DIY Candy Eyes (page 91)

Bake the cookies:

1. Preheat the oven to 375°F.

2. Place the butter in a small pot and set it to medium heat. Brown the butter until it begins to smell nutty and becomes a deep brown color. Remove it from the heat and allow it to cool for about 5 minutes.

3. In a large bowl, combine the brown sugar, rolled oats, vanilla extract, and egg, mixing well until combined. Add a couple drops of black food coloring. Gradually add the brown butter, mixing until combined.

4. Add the salt and flour and mix until combined.

5. Line a baking sheet with parchment paper. Dollop tablespoon-sized rounds of dough onto the baking sheet, spacing them about 2 inches apart, as they will spread during baking.

6. Bake for 6 minutes, then cool on the baking sheet for 5 to 8 minutes, until they have cooled slightly. Use a spatula to transfer them to a cooling rack. They'll still be delicate at this point, but the cooling rack will help them firm up. Then cool completely.

Make the dip:

1. In a large bowl, combine the cream cheese, confectioners' sugar, and vanilla extract. Beat on medium speed with an electric mixer until smooth and incorporated.

2. In a separate bowl, beat the heavy cream on medium/high speed until stiff peaks form. Add this to the cream cheese mixture and gently fold to combine.

3. Add the fresh strawberries and chocolate chips and fold to combine.

4. Spoon this into a serving bowl, then dollop the raspberry jam on top. Swirl it with a knife or spoon, then decorate with the candy eyes.

5. Serve with the cookies and enjoy!

Meringue Bone Cookies

4 large egg whites, room
   temperature
½ teaspoon cream of tartar
Pinch of salt
1 cup granulated sugar
1 teaspoon vanilla extract

1. Preheat the oven to 225°F. Line a large cookie sheet with parchment paper and set aside.

2. Place the egg whites, cream of tartar, and salt into a large mixing bowl. Beat with an electric mixer on low speed until the eggs look foamy. The mixing bowl and the whisks must be completely clean and grease-free, as the egg whites will not whip otherwise.

3. Increase the speed to high and add the granulated sugar 1 tablespoon at a time, until all of the sugar has been added and is dissolved. You'll know that the sugar has dissolved if you rub a small amount of meringue between your fingers and do not feel any graininess. Beat until the meringue is thick and glossy and holds stiff peaks.

4. Add the vanilla extract and gently stir to combine.

5. Place the meringue into a piping bag fitted with a large round piping tip.

6. To create the bones, pipe a heart onto the baking sheet, then pipe a long line extending from the base of the heart. At the base, pipe another heart, connecting its base to the long line. You can get creative and make curved bones or try to mimic real bones!

7. Bake them in the oven for 1 hour. Once they've finished baking, do not open the oven! Keep them in the oven with the door closed for 2 hours, until they are cooled completely. They will be crisp and will easily peel up from the parchment paper.

8. Store them in an airtight container and enjoy!

Pumpkin Pie Hummus

SERVES 8 TO 10

1 (15-ounce) can chickpeas, drained and rinsed
1¼ cups pure pumpkin puree (not pumpkin pie filling)
¼ cup almond butter
2 tablespoons brown sugar
2½ teaspoons Pumpkin Pie Spice (page 83)
1 teaspoon vanilla extract
Sliced apples
Teddy Grahams
Graham crackers

1. Place the chickpeas, pumpkin puree, almond butter, brown sugar, pumpkin pie spice, and vanilla extract into a food processor and pulse until smooth.

2. Scoop it into a bowl of your choice and serve with the sliced apples, Teddy Grahams, and graham crackers!

Sugar Skulls

MAKES ABOUT 5 (1-INCH) SKULLS

The spookiest way to sweeten your tea and coffee! These can take some time to dry out, depending on the humidity of your house, so if you are making these for a specific event, I recommend making them several days in advance. They will last indefinitely once made! The addition of cinnamon adds a festive flavor, but you can omit the cinnamon if you like or replace it with Pumpkin Pie Spice (page 83).

½ cup granulated sugar (or brown sugar)
½ teaspoon ground cinnamon
1 teaspoon water

1. Mix together the granulated sugar and cinnamon. Add the water and mix until it feels like damp sand. It seems like a very small amount of water, but I promise that this is all you need!

2. Using a small spoon, press the sugar into *both* sides of a 3D skull ice cube mold. Press down very, very firmly.

3. Once you feel like the sugar is firmly packed together, quickly and gently join the two sides of the mold together. The sugar may shift slightly, but as long as it stays within the skull section of the mold, it will work! Press the top of the mold very firmly from the outside, pressing both sides of the sugar together to create one solid mass.

4. Allow the mold to sit, closed, for at least 24 hours to dry out. It will take longer than usual sugar cubes, as the mold will slow this process.

5. Gently remove the top of the mold and touch one of the skulls. If it still feels damp or malleable, allow the sugar cubes to continue drying without the top half of the mold for another 12 to 24 hours. The skulls should feel as hard and dry as classic sugar cubes.

6. Then gently unmold the skulls and enjoy!

Worm-Filled Birthday Cake

SERVES 6 TO 8

1 recipe chocolate cake from Witch's Birthday Cake (page 131), baked in 4 layers

Worms:

2 boxes raspberry Jell-O
3 packets (3 tablespoons) powdered gelatin
3 cups boiling water
¾ cup heavy cream
15 drops green liquid food coloring
100 flexible straws
Mason jar
Elastic band
¼ cup Oreo cookie crumbs

Buttercream:

3 cups unsalted butter, room temperature
3 teaspoons vanilla extract
6 cups confectioners' sugar
Blue and pink food coloring

Make the worms:

1. Combine the Jell-O powder and powdered gelatin in a large bowl. Add the boiling water and stir until dissolved. Place the bowl in the fridge for 20 minutes, or until lukewarm.

2. In a separate bowl, combine the heavy cream and green food coloring. Add to the Jell-O mixture and mix well.

3. Extend the flexible straws and insert them into a tall mason jar, flexible ends downward. The straws should fit snugly into the jar. Wrap an elastic band around the straws, then slowly pour the jelly into the straws. It will pour out into the mason jar as well, but don't worry! Keep pouring until the mason jar is full. Place the jar into the fridge and leave overnight.

4. Gently pull the straws out of the mason jar (this may take a little wiggling). Working with one straw at a time, run it under hot water, then squeeze one end and push the worm out onto a plate. Repeat with the remaining straws, then place in the fridge while you assemble the cake.

Make the buttercream:

1. Beat the butter with an electric mixer until pale and fluffy. Add the vanilla extract and mix until combined.

2. Add the confectioners' sugar 1 cup at a time, mixing after each addition. Then beat the buttercream for an additional 3 to 5 minutes, until light and fluffy.

3. Dye ⅓ of the buttercream pink and the remaining ⅔ blue. Place the pink buttercream into a piping bag fitted with a large star-shaped piping tip.

(Continued . . .)

Assemble and decorate:

1. Use a serrated knife to flatten the tops of the chocolate cakes. Use a 3-inch round cookie cutter to cut the center out of 3 of the layers. Save one of the cut-out centers.

2. Place the layer without the center cut out onto the cake stand. Spread some blue buttercream on top in a ring, avoiding the middle. This is so that the worms don't stick to it

3. Layer the remaining cakes on top, spreading buttercream just on the top of the cakes and not onto the inside of the hole.

4. Fill the hole with the worms. You can toss the worms in a little bit of Oreo cookie crumbs to prevent them from sticking to each other. Don't add too many cookie crumbs, however, because they stick *too* well to the worms and can hide the color and texture of the worms.

5. Seal the hole in the cake with the reserved circle cake center. If you find that there are too many worms inside the cake to fully push the cake circle into the hole, don't press the cake in! Simply slice a little off the top of the cake circle so that the top of the cake is flat.

6. Coat the cake in a thin, even layer of buttercream. This is called a crumb coat, and it will trap all of the crumbs within this layer of buttercream and prevent them from showing on the surface. Chill the cake in the fridge for 15 minutes, for the buttercream to slightly stiffen.

7. Coat the entire cake in a thicker layer of the blue buttercream. Then use the pink buttercream to pipe dollops on the top of the cake, as well as along the base of the cake.

8. Then slice and disgust all of your guests as worms fall out of the cake!

Black Cat Candy Apples

MAKES 6 APPLES

Long lollipop sticks
6 Granny Smith apples
12 jumbo marshmallows
14 ounces caramel candies
2 tablespoons milk
2 cups black candy melts, melted (or dark chocolate)
1 tablespoon orange candy melts, melted
1 tablespoon pink candy melts, melted

1. Stick the lollipop sticks into the top of the apples. Use scissors to cut the marshmallows into ears by first trimming a thin amount of marshmallow off the flat base of each marshmallow—this will create a sticky base that will allow them to stick to the apples. Then cut two diagonal slices up from the base, creating a triangle. Stick these onto the apples. Then place the apples onto a baking sheet lined with parchment paper.

2. Place the caramels and milk into a pot and set to medium heat. Keep stirring until the candies have fully melted.

3. Turn off the heat and wait for the caramel to stop bubbling. Dip each apple into the caramel sauce, coating right up to the base of the marshmallows. If you'd like the apples to be completely coated in caramel, attach the marshmallow ears after the apples have been dipped in caramel and cooled. Place the apples on the baking sheet to set.

4. If any bubbles appear on the caramel, simply poke them with a sharp knife and deflate them.

5. Once the caramel has hardened, dip each apple into the melted black candy melts (or dark chocolate). Allow any excess chocolate to drip off. There shouldn't be too much chocolate on each apple, just enough to evenly coat the surface.

6. Allow the chocolate to set, then use a toothpick to draw the eyes with the orange candy melts, the nose with the pink candy melts, and the whiskers with the leftover black candy melts.

7. Place the apples in the fridge to set, then enjoy!

Eyeball Mochi Skewers

Syrup:
1 cup granulated sugar
½ cup water
1½ cups frozen strawberries

Mochi:
1⅓ cup shiratamako rice flour
⅔ cup + 2 tablespoons water
Red, green, blue, brown, and black
   food coloring

Make the bloody syrup:

1. Place the granulated sugar and water in a small pot and set to medium heat. Heat, while stirring, until the sugar has dissolved, about 1 minute.

2. Add the strawberries and cook for about 10 to 12 minutes, until the strawberries are very soft and the syrup is bubbling and thick.

3. Strain the syrup into a jar and set aside to cool. The leftover syrupy strawberries can be eaten with yogurt, pancakes, or waffles!

Make the eyeballs:

1. Place the shiratamako flour into a bowl, and gradually drizzle in the water. Knead with a spoon (or your hands—much easier). The dough should form into one piece, and be firm enough for a piece of dough to be rolled into a ball, and retain its form when placed down. Depending on the humidity of your house, you may need to add a bit more flour or water, but do so very gradually.

2. Take ¼ of the dough and divide it into 5 pieces. Dye it red, green, blue, brown, and black. Keep in mind that the dough will get deeper in color once it is boiled.

3. Roll the remaining dough into 8 balls and place it on a plate lined with plastic wrap. The dough will easily stick to plates and countertops and the plastic wrap will prevent this.

4. Create the iris of the eyes with the brown, green, blue, and red dough by making little disks of the dough and pressing them onto the white balls. To make the pupils, make little balls with the black dough and press them into the center of the iris.

(Continued . . .)

5. To cook the eyeballs, bring a large pot of water to boil. Add the eyeballs. Once they have risen to the surface, boil for 3 to 5 minutes, until cooked al the way through. Immediately transfer the eyeballs to a bowl of ice water, to stop the cooking and prevent them from getting too soft.

Serve:

1. Stick the eyeballs onto skewers and place on a serving plate.

2. Drizzle the strawberry "blood" on top and enjoy!

VAMPIRE'S LAIR

Vampire Hot Chocolate

SERVES 2

¼ cup dark chocolate, melted
3.5 ounces high-quality white
   chocolate
2 cups milk
Red food coloring
2 cups heavy cream
¼ cup confectioners' sugar
1 teaspoon vanilla extract
Black food coloring
Edible Blood (page 175)

1. Prep the mugs by drizzling the dark chocolate along the outside of both mugs. Place the mugs in the freezer for 5 to 10 minutes, for the chocolate to harden. Then set aside.

2. Place the white chocolate and the milk into a pot and set to medium heat. Stir continuously until the white chocolate melts, about 5 minutes. Add a couple drops of red food coloring until it reaches your desired shade of red. Set aside.

3. To make the whipped topping, place the heavy cream, confectioners' sugar, vanilla extract, and a very tiny drop of black food coloring into a large bowl and beat with an electric mixer until stiff peaks form.

4. Place the cream into a piping bag fitted with a large star-shaped piping tip.

5. Fill the mugs with the hot chocolate and pipe a swirl of whipped cream on top. Use a spoon to drop 2 droplets of edible blood onto the edge of the cream, to look like a vampire bite.

6. Serve and enjoy!

Batty Ganache Tart

Tart crust:

12 ounces Oreo cookies
11 tablespoons (½ cup +
   3 tablespoons) melted, unsalted
   butter
1 batch cookie dough from Black Cat
   Cookies (page 123)

Blueberry ganache:

4 ounces frozen blueberries,
   thawed with juices remaining (use
   2 teaspoons of the juice)
7 ounces white chocolate, finely
   chopped
⅓ cup heavy cream
Blue food coloring (optional)

Raspberry ganache:

4 ounces frozen raspberries, thawed
   with juices remaining (use
   2 teaspoons of the juice)
7 ounces white chocolate, finely
   chopped
⅓ cup heavy cream
Pink food coloring, optional

Make the crust:

1. Place the Oreo cookies in a food processor and pulse until they resemble a fine crumb.

2. Add the melted butter and pulse until fully incorporated.

3. Press the crust into the bottom and sides of a 10-inch tart pan with a removable bottom.

4. Place the crust into the fridge to chill while you make the other components.

Make the bats:

1. Preheat the oven to 350°F. Roll the dough out on a floured surface to ¼-inch thick. Use various sizes of bat cookie cutters and cut out cookies.

2. Place the cookies on a baking sheet lined with parchment paper and bake for 10 minutes, until the edges are just starting to brown. Cool completely.

Make the ganache:

1. Start with the blueberry ganache. Place the blueberries into a blender and pulse until smooth. Pass them through a sieve to remove any skin and seeds. Set aside.

2. In a small pot, combine the white chocolate and cream over low heat. Stir frequently until the chocolate has fully melted. Remove the pan from the heat, add the blueberry puree, and stir to combine. If desired, add a couple drops of blue food coloring.

3. Pour the ganache into a bowl and set aside.

(Continued . . .)

4. Repeat these steps for the raspberry ganache, adding some pink food coloring at the end, if desired.

5. Allow both flavors of ganache to chill in the fridge long enough for them to thicken slightly, but still be pourable, at least 10 minutes.

Assemble:

1. Hold the bowls of ganache over either side of the tart and pour them into the tart crust at the same time. Half of the tart should be blueberry ganache and the other side should be raspberry ganache.

2. Use a butter knife to swirl the edges of the ganache together, to create a sunset effect.

3. Place the tart in the fridge until the ganache has set, at least 1 hour.

4. Once the ganache has set, place the bat cookies on top, then slice and serve!

Vampire Double Chocolate Cookies

Cookie dough:

3 ounces unsweetened chocolate,
  roughly chopped
1 cup dark chocolate chips
½ cup unsalted butter
3 large eggs
1 cup + 2 tablespoons granulated
  sugar
Black food coloring
¾ cup all-purpose flour
⅓ teaspoon baking powder
¼ teaspoon salt

Chocolate ganache and decorations:

8 ounces white chocolate, melted
Pinch of salt
¾ cup heavy cream, hot
Red food coloring
2 cups mini marshmallows
Slivered almonds

Bake the cookies:

1. Preheat the oven to 350°F. Place the unsweetened chocolate, dark chocolate chips, and butter into a pot set to medium-low heat, and stir until everything is melted.

2. Place the eggs and sugar in a bowl and whisk on high speed with an electric mixer until it forms a ribbon when lifted, about 3 minutes.

3. Add the chocolate mixture to the eggs and sugar while whisking. Add a couple drops of black food coloring and mix until incorporated.

4. Sift the flour, baking powder, and salt into the bowl and mix just until everything is combined.

5. Line a baking sheet with parchment paper and place tablespoon-sized balls of dough about 2 inches apart. Bake for 10 to 12 minutes.

6. Allow the cookies to cool for 1 minute, then transfer them to a cooling rack to cool completely.

Make the ganache:

1. Combine the melted white chocolate, salt, and heavy cream in a bowl. Add a couple drops of red food coloring. Place in the fridge until the ganache has cooled and thickened.

2. Beat the ganache with an electric mixer until it slightly lightens in color and becomes creamy and a whipped consistency.

3. Place in a piping bag fitted with a large round tip.

(Continued . . .)

Assemble:

1. Match up the cookies so that you have pairs of cookies that are a similar size and shape.

2. Turn one cookie upside down and pipe a thin layer of ganache onto the flat size of the cookie. Place a ring of marshmallows around the edge of the cookie. Pipe some additional ganache onto the bottom of the other cookie and place this on top of the cookie with marshmallows. Stick 2 almond slivers into the "teeth" to create the fangs.

3. Place the cookie on a plate and in the fridge to chill while you assemble the remaining cookies. This will prevent the ganache from slipping or dripping.

4. Serve and enjoy!

Bat Cookies

Cookie dough:

2 cups all-purpose flour
¼ teaspoon salt
½ teaspoon baking powder
½ cup unsalted butter, room
    temperature
1 cup granulated sugar
2 tablespoons milk
1 large egg
½ teaspoon vanilla extract

Icing and decorations:

1 batch Royal Icing (page 177)
Brown food coloring
1 cup brown sprinkles
DIY Candy Eyes (page 91)

Bake the cookies:

1. Preheat the oven to 350°F.

2. Mix together the flour, salt, and baking powder in a bowl. In a separate bowl, cream the butter and sugar with an electric mixer until it becomes light and fluffy.

3. Add the milk, egg, and vanilla extract. Mix until well combined, then add the flour mixture and mix until just combined.

4. Shape the dough into a ball and wrap in plastic wrap. Chill it in the fridge for 1 hour, until firm.

5. Roll the cookie dough out on a floured surface to a ¼-inch thickness. Use a bat-shaped cookie cutter to cut out cookies and place them on a baking sheet lined with parchment paper.

6. Bake them for 10 minutes, then transfer to a wire rack and cool completely.

Decorate:

1. Dye ¾ of the Royal Icing a dark brown color. Place it into a piping bag fitted with a small round piping tip.

2. Pipe an outline around just the wings of the bat first and fill them in with more brown icing. Allow this to dry completely, about 2 hours.

3. Using the same brown icing, pipe an outline around the bats' head and body and fill in the outline with more icing. Dunk the cookie into the brown sprinkles, so that the sprinkles stick to the wet icing.

4. While the body is drying, pipe the details onto the bat wings with more icing. Then attach 2 candy eyes to each bat with more brown frosting.

5. Place the remaining white icing into a piping bag fitted with a small round piping tip. Pipe two fangs onto each bat. This can be done before the body is finished drying, as the sprinkles will prevent the white fangs from bleeding into the brown base.

6. Allow the icing to dry completely, about 6 to 12 hours. Then enjoy!

Bat Marshmallow Pops

MAKES 5 BATS

5 jumbo marshmallows
10 chocolate chips
5 lollipop sticks
3 Oreo cookies
1 cup melted dark chocolate
10 DIY Candy Eyes (page 91)

1. Use scissors to cut off a very small slice of marshmallow from the top of each marshmallow. This will create a sticky surface. Stick 2 chocolate chips onto the top of the marshmallow, creating the bat's ears.

2. Skewer each marshmallow onto a lollipop stick

3. Line a baking sheet with parchment paper. Set aside. Separate the Oreo cookies and remove the cream filling. Carefully break each cookie in half, creating a half moon shape. You will need 2 half moon shapes per bat. Arrange the cookies in groups of 2 on the baking sheet to look like wings.

4. Submerge the marshmallows in the melted dark chocolate. Allow any excess chocolate to drip off, then lay the marshmallow flat onto the Oreo wings. Repeat with all the marshmallows, then stick 2 candy eyes onto each bat.

5. Place the tray in the fridge for the chocolate to set, about 30 minutes. Serve and enjoy!

Vampire Gingerbread Men

Cookies:
2 cups all-purpose flour
2 teaspoons ground ginger
1 teaspoon ground cinnamon
½ teaspoon ground nutmeg
¼ teaspoon ground cloves
¼ teaspoon baking soda
¼ teaspoon salt
½ cup unsalted butter, room
    temperature
⅓ cup brown sugar
⅓ cup molasses
1 large egg, room temperature
5 lollipop sticks

Icing and decorations:
2 cups Royal Icing (page 177)
Black food coloring
Red and purple sprinkles
Red edible ink pen

Bake the cookies:
1. Preheat the oven to 350°F.

2. Combine the flour, ginger, cinnamon, nutmeg, cloves, baking soda, and salt. Set aside.

3. In a separate bowl, beat the butter and brown sugar with an electric mixer until light and fluffy. Add the molasses and egg and mix well.

4. Add the dry ingredients and mix until just combined.

5. Shape the dough into a ball and wrap in plastic wrap. Chill in the fridge for at least 1 hour, until firm.

6. Flour the work surface and roll the dough out until it is ⅛- to ¼-inch thick. Use a gingerbread man cookie cutter to cut out cookies and place them on a baking sheet lined with parchment paper.

7. Bake for 10 minutes, until the edges are just starting to brown. Cool completely.

Decorate:
1. Dye 1½ cups of Royal Icing black and place it in a piping bag fitted with a small round piping tip. Place the white Royal Icing into a piping bag also fitted with a small round piping tip.

2. Use the black Royal Icing to pipe the faces onto the cookies. Use some extra icing to stick the red and purple "buttons" to the cookies.

3. Use the white Royal Icing to pipe the fangs. Let dry completely, 3 to 4 hours.

4. Use the red edible ink pen to draw a little touch of red at the point of the fangs, to look like blood!

Edible Blood

MAKES ABOUT ½ CUP

½ cup clear corn syrup
2 teaspoons cornstarch
Red food coloring
Blue food coloring

1. Combine the corn syrup and cornstarch together in a bowl. The cornstarch will thicken the blood, so add as little or as much as you like!

2. Add enough red food coloring to achieve a deep red shade. Add the tiniest amount of blue food coloring—around ¼ of a drop. This will add depth to the red, but not make it turn purple.

3. Apply to your desired cake, candies, or cookies! To store, simply place in a sealed plastic container and store in the fridge.

Spiderweb Cookies

MAKES 1 DOZEN COOKIES

Cookie dough:

2 cups all-purpose flour
¼ teaspoon salt
½ teaspoon baking powder
½ cup unsalted butter, room
   temperature
1 cup granulated sugar
2 tablespoons milk
1 large egg
½ teaspoon vanilla extract
Black food coloring

Royal icing and decorations:

¾ cup warm water
5 tablespoons meringue powder
1 teaspoon cream of tartar
2.2 pounds confectioners' sugar
Lemon extract, or any clear extract
   that isn't too potent in flavor.
   (Vodka also works!)
Red and black food coloring
1 teaspoon black edible glitter

Bake the cookies:

1. Mix together the flour, salt, and baking powder in a bowl.

2. In a separate bowl, cream the butter and sugar with an electric mixer until it becomes light and fluffy. Add the milk, egg, vanilla, and several drops of black food coloring and mix well.

3. Slowly add the dry ingredients and mix until just combined.

4. Shape the dough into a ball, wrap in plastic wrap, and chill in the fridge for 1 hour.

5. Roll the dough on a floured surface until it is ¼-inch thick. Use a 3-inch round cookie cutter to cut out the cookies and place them on a baking sheet lined with parchment paper.

6. Bake the cookies at 350°F for 10 minutes, until the edges are just starting to brown.

7. Once they are removed from the oven, place another sheet of parchment paper on top of the cookies, followed by another baking sheet. Press down firmly. This will flatten any tops of cookies that have risen and ensure that the tops are smooth and flat. Remove the additional baking sheet and parchment paper and cool the cookies completely.

Make the royal icing:

1. Pour the warm water into a large bowl. Add the meringue powder and whisk for a couple seconds until frothy. Add the cream of tartar and whisk again.

2. Add the confectioners' sugar all at once and using an electric mixer, mix on low speed for 10 minutes. The icing should stay on the surface for 5 to 7 seconds when drizzled. Add the lemon extract and mix well.

(Continued . . .)

3. Divide the icing into 2 bowls. Leave one bowl white and dye the other bowl black.

4. Place the icing into piping bags fitted with small round piping tips.

Decorate:

1. Working with one cookie at a time, pipe an outer circle of black icing onto the cookie, just slightly inside the outer edge of the cookie. You want to leave a little bit of room for dragging the icing outward.

2. Fill in the circle with black icing.

3. As soon as the circle is full, take the white icing and pipe a dollop in the center of the cookie. Pipe concentric circles of white icing around the dollop, leaving some space in between each circle.

4. Take a toothpick and begin to drag it through the icing, starting at the center dollop and making lines outward to the edge of the cookie. Only drag from the middle outward, otherwise the cobweb will look more like a flower! You may want to wipe excess icing off the toothpick in between each line you make, so that the colors don't begin to blend together.

5. Repeat with the remaining cookies, then allow the cookies to dry at room temperature for about 6 hours or overnight.

6. You can stop at this point, but if you'd like to add spiders, do so now while the cookies are drying! Line a baking sheet with parchment paper and pipe spiders with the remaining black icing. Allow them to dry until they are completely firm, about 2 to 3 hours. They will take less time to harden than the cookies because of the smaller surface area.

7. Once the spiders have dried, take a small dish and combine 1 teaspoon of black edible glitter with 1 to 2 drops of lemon extract. Mix until the glitter has dissolved and looks like metallic, liquidy paint.

8. Use a clean paintbrush to paint the glitter onto the spiders. Allow the paint to dry to the touch at room temperature, then set aside until the base cookies have dried.

9. Gently peel the spiders off the parchment paper and use a tiny amount of excess icing as glue to attach them to the web cookies. Enjoy!

Mummy Hot Chocolate Bombs

These mummies are made from white chocolate, however they are filled with a classic hot chocolate mix, so if you're not a huge fan of white chocolate, don't worry! It still tastes like classic hot chocolate, just with a creamier touch. To serve, place each hot chocolate bomb in a mug and top with 1 to 2 cups of hot milk.

Shells:

12 ounces high-quality white
   chocolate

Filling and decorations:

3 tablespoons cocoa powder
6 tablespoons granulated sugar
3 tablespoons mini marshmallows
6 DIY Candy Eyes (page 91)

Make the shells:

1. Break the chocolate into small pieces and place it in a microwave-safe bowl. Microwave it for 20- to 30-second intervals, mixing at each interval. The chocolate can also be melted using a double boiler.

2. Fill a hot chocolate bomb mold ¾ of the way full with the chocolate and gently rotate it so that the chocolate coats all sides. Place a sheet of parchment paper onto the work surface. Turn the mold upside down and allow the excess chocolate to drip onto the parchment paper. Scrape the chocolate off the parchment paper and return it to the bowl.

3. Use the flat back of a butter knife to smooth the edges of the chocolate mold. Place the mold in the fridge for 20 to 30 minutes, until the chocolate has fully set.

4. Repeat steps 2 and 3, to create a second layer of chocolate. This will prevent the chocolate shell from breaking during unmolding and assembly. When smoothing the edges of the chocolate mold with the butter knife, ensure that the edges of the shell are 1 to 3 millimeters thick. This will allow both halves to securely stick together in the following steps.

5. Gently unmold the chocolate shells and rest them on a plate or on top of small glasses, which will support the spherical shape very well and keep it from wobbling away

(Continued . . .)

6. Pour some boiling water into a bowl and place a plate on top. The heat of the boiling water will heat up the plate. Once the plate feels warm to the touch, place once shell at a time onto the plate, curved-side up. Allow the edges of the shell to melt very slightly, then lift off the plate. This will create a flat edge on the shells and will make assembly MUCH easier. Set this contraption aside, as you will need it again to assemble.

Make the filling:

1. Combine the cocoa powder, sugar, and marshmallows in a small bowl.

Assembly:

1. Spoon some of the mix into one chocolate shell. You don't have to use all of the mixture. Add some marshmallows and sprinkles, if desired.

2. Take an empty shell and place it back on the heated plate and bowl from step 6. Allow it to just start to the melt the edges of the shell, then place it onto the filled shell. This will melt the edges of the shell to create a "glue" to seal both sides together!

3. Run your finger along the seam to remove any excess chocolate and seal the two shells together.

4. Set aside and continue with the remaining shells.

5. Place the remaining chocolate into a piping bag and snip a small hole at the end. Drizzle the chocolate back and forth over the top of each bomb to look like bandages. Allow the chocolate to set for a couple minutes in the fridge, until it is less runny, but still sticky, and stick 2 candy eyes onto each bomb.

6. Return the bombs to the fridge to completely set, about 30 minutes. Then enjoy!

Mummy Brownies

MAKES 9 BROWNIES

Brownie batter:
8 ounces semisweet chocolate
¾ cup unsalted butter, melted
1¼ cups granulated sugar
2 large eggs, room temperature
2 teaspoons vanilla extract
¾ cup all-purpose flour
¼ cup cocoa powder
1 teaspoon salt

Frosting and decorations:
1 cup unsalted butter, room
   temperature
1 teaspoon vanilla extract
3 cups confectioners' sugar
18 DIY Candy Eyes (page 91)

Bake the brownies:
1. Preheat the oven to 350°F.

2. Chop the chocolate into small pieces and place in a microwave-safe bowl. Microwave for 30-second intervals, stirring at each interval, until melted. Set aside.

3. In a large bowl, beat the butter and sugar with an electric mixer until light and fluffy. Add the eggs and vanilla and mix until well combined. Add the melted chocolate and mix well.

4. Add the flour, cocoa powder, and salt and use a spatula to fold to combine.

5. Pour the batter into an 8 × 8-inch square baking dish that has been lined with parchment paper.

6. Bake for about 25 minutes, then place the dish on a wire rack and allow the brownies to cool completely in the dish

Make the frosting:
1. Place the butter in a large bowl and beat with an electric mixer until light and fluffy. Add the vanilla extract and mix until combined.

2. Add the confectioners' sugar 1 cup at a time, mixing until combined, then beat for 2 to 3 minutes, until light and fluffy.

3. Place the frosting into a piping bag fitted with a #45 flat piping tip. This will make the frosting look like flat bandages!

Decorate:
1. Use a sharp knife to cut the brownie into 9 even squares.

2. Use the frosting to pipe a zigzag pattern across the entire surface of the brownies.

3. Stick two candy eyes on top of each brownie and enjoy!

Ghost Macarons

If you don't have access to superfine sugar, place some granulated sugar in a food processor and pulse until it is more finely ground! Measure the sugar as this point, after grinding, not before, as the volume may change.

Macarons:

1 cup confectioners' sugar
¾ cup almond flour (not almond meal)
2 large egg whites
Pinch of cream of tartar
¼ cup superfine sugar

Decorations:

1 cup hazelnut spread
Black edible ink pen

Make the macarons:

1. Combine the confectioners' sugar and almond flour in a bowl, then sift 3 times.

2. Place the egg whites in a large bowl and beat with an electric mixer until foamy. Add the cream of tartar, then beat until soft peaks form. Add the superfine sugar and beat on high speed until stiff peaks form. Sift the dry mixture into the egg mixture and gently fold to combine.

3. Line a baking sheet with parchment paper. Place the batter in a piping bag fitted with large round tip and pipe 1-inch rounds, then drag the piping bag downward to create the tail of the ghosts. Be sure to make ghosts that have tails going both right and left, as you need a mirroring ghost for the back of each macaron!

4. Wet your finger with water and smooth the top of the macarons. Tap the baking sheets on the countertop a couple times to remove any air bubbles. Let the macarons sit at room temperature for 30 minutes.

5. Set the oven to 375°F, heat for 5 minutes, then reduce the heat to 325°F. Bake the macarons, one sheet at a time, for 6 to 8 minutes, rotating halfway through. After each batch, increase the heat to 375°F, heat for 5 minutes, then reduce to 325°F and pop the next sheet into the oven!

6. Allow the macarons to cool on the sheet for 2 to 3 minutes, then transfer to a wire rack to fully cool.

To assemble:

1. Place the hazelnut spread into a piping bag and snip off the end to create a small piping tip. Flip the macarons over and pipe some ganache around the border of half the macarons. Then place another macaron on top.

2. Use the black edible ink pen to draw the ghost's eyes and mouth. Press down gently as macaron shells are delicate! Enjoy!

Metric Conversions

If you're accustomed to using metric measurements, use these handy charts to convert the imperial measurements used in this book.

Weight (Dry Ingredients)

1 oz		30 g
4 oz	¼ lb	120 g
8 oz	½ lb	240 g
12 oz	¾ lb	360 g
16 oz	1 lb	480 g
32 oz	2 lb	960 g

Oven Temperatures

Fahrenheit	Celsius	Gas Mark
225°	110°	¼
250°	120°	½
275°	140°	1
300°	150°	2
325°	160°	3
350°	180°	4
375°	190°	5
400°	200°	6
425°	220°	7
450°	230°	8

Volume (Liquid Ingredients)

½ tsp.		2 ml
1 tsp.		5 ml
1 Tbsp.	½ fl oz	15 ml
2 Tbsp.	1 fl oz	30 ml
¼ cup	2 fl oz	60 ml
⅓ cup	3 fl oz	80 ml
½ cup	4 fl oz	120 ml
⅔ cup	5 fl oz	160 ml
¾ cup	6 fl oz	180 ml
1 cup	8 fl oz	240 ml
1 pt	16 fl oz	480 ml
1 qt	32 fl oz	960 ml

Length

¼ in	6 mm
½ in	13 mm
¾ in	19 mm
1 in	25 mm
6 in	15 cm
12 in	30 cm

Index

Also Available

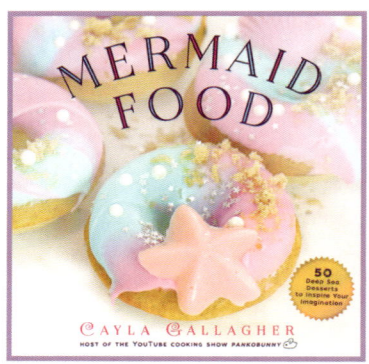